Boos

Boost your child's confidence

52 brilliant drama techniques
to help your child shine

Lucy Morgans & Steve Hemsley

brilliantideas

CAREFUL NOW

Few people can be bothered to read the small print in any book. Luckily there isn't much when it comes to using drama techniques and games to make children more confident.

All the publishers and your friendly authors will say is don't expect miracles overnight because every child is different. We don't know you or your child personally, but what we do know is that these ideas are helping to remove shyness and nervousness in kids up and down the country. Hopefully they will work for your family too and you'll have great fun in the process.

If they don't work immediately keep trying because often these exercises need regular practice and lots of patience before results are seen.

But don't forget to talk to your health practitioner if you feel there are deeper issues affecting your child's confidence either at home or at school.

Copyright © The Infinite Ideas Company Limited, 2008

The right of Lucy Morgans and Steve Hemsley to be identified as the authors of this book has been asserted in accordance with the Copyright, Designs and Patents Act 1988.

First published in 2008 by
The Infinite Ideas Company Limited
36 St Giles
Oxford, OX1 3LD
United Kingdom
www.infideas.com

A CIP catalogue record for this book is available from the British Library

ISBN 978-1-905940-47-9

Brand and product names are trademarks or registered trademarks of their respective owners.
The authors would like to thank Phillip Young and Craig Peters for kindly allowing us to use the photos on pages 5, 9, 13, 14, 33, 38, 47, 48, 69, 74, 87, 96, 101, 105, 109, 114, 120, 139, 143, 147, 151, 155, 159, 164, 165, 169, 173, 177, 181, 186, 187, 191, 199, 203, 207, 211, 219, 223, 228 and 233.

Designed by Baseline Arts Ltd, Oxford
Typeset by Sparks
Printed in India

Brilliant ideas

1 **Who says life's not a rehearsal?** 1
   Wouldn't it be wonderful to go through life making mistakes with no one really caring?
   Unfortunately that is never going to happen so remember practice makes perfect – well,
   almost.

2 **The ins and outs of breathing** 5
   When children get nervous their breathing becomes shaky and their mouths dry up. If
   they learn to breathe correctly they can take on the world.

3 **Manners maketh man (and child)** 9
   Theatre etiquette means actors understand the importance of listening, when to be
   quiet and why they must be considerate to others on stage. These are skills children can
   benefit from enormously.

4 **Prop till you drop** 15
   Don't tell the cleaning police, but clutter is good. Items strewn around the house provide
   actors with props that add reality to a scene while they can fire a child's imagination.

5 **How Now Brown Cow** 19
   No-one expects your child to sound like a 1940s BBC public service broadcast, but if he
   can express himself confidently people will listen to what he has to say.

Brilliant features

Each chapter of this book is designed to provide you with an inspirational idea that you can read quickly and put into practice straight away.

Throughout you'll find four features that will help you get right to the heart of the idea:

- *Here's an idea for you ...* Take it on board and give it a go – right here, right now. Get an idea of how well you're doing so far.

- *Try another idea ...* If this idea looks like a life-changer then there's no time to lose. *Try another idea ...* will point you straight to a related tip to enhance and expand on the first.

- *Defining idea ...* Words of wisdom from masters and mistresses of the art, plus some interesting hangers-on.

- *How did it go?* If at first you do succeed, try to hide your amazement. If, on the other hand, you don't, then this is where you'll find a Q and A that highlights common problems and how to solve them.

Introduction

Growing up is a tough business. The road to independence can seem an arduous one and it's natural for parents to want to take control, hold the map and give directions.

Unfortunately, if we're too overprotective our children will lack the confidence to ask questions, trust others, try new things or make mistakes, which ultimately they'll learn from.

A shy or nervous child won't make the most of every opportunity. If she has more confidence she'll blossom in social situations and make more friends, and prosper at school as she grows into a balanced and self-assured young adult.

This book contains 52 drama-based ideas that, with a little perseverance, will transform your retiring wallflower into the outgoing and happy child you know he or she can be.

We're revealing the secrets of the acting world here by unveiling techniques that thespians across the globe use day after day to remove nerves, help them to interact with other characters and generally feel more comfortable in their bodies.

If you think about it, the whole essence of being an actor is having the confidence to stand up on your own and be noticed in front of an expectant and potentially critical audience. How scary is that?

By unlocking the actor's toolbox your child will feel he can cope with anything life throws at him. Actors are encouraged to try new things but also to focus on what they're really good at. The praise they receive and the sense of achievement they feel can be massive.

We wouldn't dare tell you how to bring up your kids and we certainly don't want you to turn into some awful pushy stage mum or dad desperate to get your offspring a lead role in Hollywood.

We just want to explain how, by using drama exercises and games in a very low-pressure and non-judgemental environment, your child will soon have much more self-belief.

She'll learn how to remain calm under pressure and improve her memory so she retains information and instructions. She'll become confident enough to accept constructive criticism and not be afraid to unleash her imagination. She'll concentrate better, make more use of her five senses and tackle phobias and fears that could be holding her back without her realising it.

These ideas have worked for hundreds of children who attend drama classes up and down the country. In more than a decade of teaching, Lucy has received a huge amount of feedback from parents. They tell her time and again how such techniques have changed their entire family's life as well as their child's.

Mums and dads have witnessed their children become more confident in how they express themselves in speech and movement, and noticed how their kids can now deal with situations that used to be incredibly daunting for them.

Increasingly, drama is being used by teachers in mainstream schools to engage children in a whole range of subjects from mathematics to history. They have realised how drama encourages kids to speak with confidence, listen, understand and contribute to class discussions.

In the Kent school where Steve is a parent governor, drama is used as a way to stimulate children's writing and to help them express their feelings. The pupils will often act out historical events or stories to help them learn before they put pen to paper.

Children as young as three can become more self-assured by trying the exercises in this book.

The great thing, however, is whatever your child's age there are ways to remove the nerves which can mean he's too scared to volunteer or absolutely terrified of reading aloud in class.

Most of the ideas can be tried almost anywhere – and they have been – whether you're bored in the car, having a meal as a family, walking to school or hosting a birthday party. These techniques have been carefully chosen so they can be tweaked to suit different scenarios, themes and locations.

The main thing is they are fun so you should not have any trouble tempting your child away from the television or the games console. He'll want to take part because most of this stuff is, well, just playing!

Let us know how you get on!

Lucy Morgans and Steve Hemsley

1

Who says life's not a rehearsal?

Wouldn't it be wonderful to go through life making mistakes with no one really caring? Unfortunately that is never going to happen so remember practice makes perfect – well, almost.

There will always be times a child will be nervous about something adults may view as trivial but to them is the most important thing in the world.

One red-faced actress recalls how two defrosted chicken fillets she used to pad out and enhance her cleavage fell out of her costume and on to the floor during rehearsals for a UK tour of *Annie*. She was mortified. The director and cast found the incident as hilarious as any of us would on finding a friend with a poultry-enhanced figure, but they wouldn't have been laughing had it happened on the opening night. Let's just say chicken was not on the menu when the curtain came up.

Rehearsals are crucial to the whole performance process. They're also a much better time to make mistakes than on the big day. Actors will run through their lines and movements until their bodies ache so they can cope with anything on stage. Children can use this most fundamental of acting techniques to prepare for situations

Here's an idea for you... **If your son is preparing for an exam where he'll be tested face-to-face, rehearse walking into a room. This is crucial. In auditions directors decide if they like an actor within seconds of meeting them. First ask your son to walk in lazily in an almost yobbish way, then to enter quietly and to say 'hello' shyly. Point out why these two approaches are not ideal and then ask him to walk in again being self-assured and polite. Next time he enters a room he'll ooze confidence and be perceived as assertive – even if deep down he's not.**

that worry them. They may be frightened about a trip to the doctor or dreading a meeting with their head teacher, so a bit of rehearsing can put a problem into perspective.

Actors rehearse because it allows them the freedom to get things wrong without an audience or theatre critic watching their every move. Similarly, whatever your child's concerns, acting out different scenarios and considering the possible outcomes will put him or her at ease.

Opticians, for instance, are often considered scary places and many young children find their first eye examination a daunting prospect. If this rings a bell with you, why not create a pretend optician at home? There's no need to buy a white coat or put your hair up to look intelligent, but you can set the scene with a few fun eye tests with letters and pictures. Take your child through every stage of the examination, from the moment she enters the shop and meets the friendly optometrist through to the tests and the fun part of trying on different pairs of glasses. Most of us have pairs of real or toy spectacles and sunglasses around the house.

By practising an event at home your child will be prepared for (virtually) every eventuality. Take the head teacher scenario. Maybe little Johnny has been accused of doing something wrong. The days of the old school cane may be long gone but the feeling of fear in the pit of the stomach and of legs turning to jelly is one any child waiting outside the head's office can relate to. Rehearsing what your child should say, how the head is likely to respond and the actions the school might take should ensure he actually sleeps the night before. It helps if you play the role of the head teacher and question him about what happened. Let him practise his answers and don't criticise his responses or force on him what you would say in his shoes. School has changed a lot since your day, Dad!

Rehearsing works better with props, which make situations more realistic and useful items can be found around the house. More on this in IDEA 4, *Prop till you drop*.

Try another idea...

Feel free to advise your child but:

- Don't put him under even more pressure because he'll be worried enough and you'll make things worse
- Keep it fun and remember this is a game and not a test.

For an interesting twist, swap roles. This will introduce some light-hearted banter to what started off as a stressful situation and help your child see things from the school's viewpoint.

The whole principle behind rehearsing is that you are free to make mistakes in a risk-free environment.

Yet getting things wrong is one of the secrets of success in life. What seems a disaster at the time is actually valuable experience. Just avoid the chicken fillets.

'Practice is the best of all instructors.'
PUBLILIUS SYRUS, Latin writer

Defining idea...

How did it go?

Q   My child was nervous about starting Brownies so we practised what might happen on her first day. Why did she still find it so difficult to mix with the other girls?

A   *Making new friends is never easy especially when a child joins a new club or organisation where many of the members already know each other very well. A child can feel overwhelmed but Girl Guiding is a great hobby, so persevere. Try rehearsing different questions and conversations she can have with the girls at Brownies. She can chat to them about their pets and family or favourite television programmes. Give your daughter plenty of ideas to help get conversations started.*

Q   That is all very well, but what if she refuses to go back to Brownies after this experience?

A   *Give your daughter examples of where it has taken time for her to settle in before and how she met the friends she has at school. With most after-school activities, attending a second time is crucial. Your child is likely to be invited to join in more at Brownies in week two and she will know what to expect having attended once already. There's no harm in practising again what might happen and focusing on what she is finding the most difficult. It would be a shame if she never went back and didn't increase her circle of friends.*

2

The ins and outs of breathing

When children get nervous their breathing becomes shaky and their mouths dry up: If your child learns to breathe correctly he or she can take on the world.

During a radio phone-in, vocal experts argued whether or not opera singers can be too fat. Heavy singers, such as the late Luciano Pavarotti, have always claimed their weight gives them better breath control before performing.

Whether this is true or not, no one is suggesting your child should start piling on the pounds to improve his chances of a career in the music industry. Yet, whatever his size, before singing or doing anything important he should heed the advice to 'take a deep breath'. Actors train hard to get their breathing right, enduring warm-up exercises before they rehearse or perform. In fact, correct breathing is one of the most important tools they use.

Without it an actor won't have enough vocal energy to complete an important speech on stage. Half an hour before the curtain rises you'll find actors practising their breathing rather than chatting in the wings. The secret to good breathing is not to breathe from your chest but to use your diaphragm so you inhale as much air as possible. A nervous child minutes away from reading or speaking aloud, or preparing to do something for the first time won't be calm if her breathing is too shallow.

Like devoted Buddhists, actors love to chant mantras when practising breathing. It is a method children can use too. Repeating phrases such as 'I am calm' or 'I can do this' helps chase away any butterflies fluttering in the stomach. Your child will learn to speak more slowly and project his voice as effectively as actors did years ago before microphones were invented. The embarrassment of sometimes having to repeat things will vanish as the pace and pitch of his speech improves and he becomes more articulate.

Here's an idea for you... **Stand opposite your child and both take a big breath aiming to use your diaphragm. Straightaway you'll see whose shoulders and upper chest are moving. Any movement should come from below the rib cage. Now start to say the months of the year. You should be able to see each other's diaphragms moving as you talk and don't be surprised if your child is better at this than you! Children are often more adaptable to new ideas than their parents.**

So, here's a quick question. Where exactly is your diaphragm? Not sure? Well, put your thumb on your last rib and place your hands flat on the bottom of your stomach. If you are breathing wrongly your shoulders will rise up and down. Now move your furniture. Stay with us on this one. The best way to practise is to lie on your back on the floor, breathe in for a count of eight and out for the count of eight. Try it again standing up but don't tip your chin upwards because this will trap the air trying to escape. Like a good burp after a heavy Chinese meal, air needs a direct route out of the body!

Be careful how you practise with your child. At one drama class the children were asked to take a deep breath and hold a 'humming' sound for as long as they could. The winner was promised chocolate as a prize, but one lad tried so hard he almost passed out. This just goes to show you should never underestimate the appeal of sweets, or the lengths kids will go to get them!

Try these games instead:

■ Ask your child to pretend she's picking up a dandelion and to blow away the seeds.
■ Take a deep breath and see how far through the alphabet your child can get before breathing again.
■ Can he 'baa' like a sheep or pant like a dog? This gets the diaphragm working really hard.
■ To make children aware of the volume of their voice get them to say words quietly or loudly. Five is noisy and one means softly. Ask them to say 'yes' in a number four voice or 'no' in a number three voice.
■ Before an important talk or speech at school practise certain sounds such as 'ttt', 'rrr' or 'vvv'.

Actors spend years perfecting the technique of perfect breathing so persevere, and don't stop eating. It might actually help.

Breathing and speech are closely related. Check out IDEA 5, *How Now Brown Cow*, all about improving speech and articulation.

Try another idea…

'As a child I mimicked teachers, but as an adult impersonating children is much more fun. Whatever sound comes out of our mouths is intrinsically linked to how we breathe.'
SUSAN SHERIDAN (voice of Noddy)

Defining idea…

How did it go?

**Q   My son is captain of the school football team. He has been prac-
tising his breathing so he can project his voice and communicate
with his teammates but how do I stop him still coming home
sounding hoarse?**

*A   He is probably still not breathing correctly. Get him to practise at home
standing with his hand on his diaphragm and his chin at a 90-degree angle
with his neck to ensure he does not strain his vocal cords. Ask him to first
say 'hello' quietly, then gaining in volume so he can observe how his voice
can travel further without straining. If his shoulders are moving he isn't
using diaphragmatic breathing. Similarly, if he's leaning forward or sticking
out his chin whilst shouting, as many of us do, he is putting too much pressure on his vocal chords.*

**Q   Hang on, what if he doesn't see any improvement after a few
weeks? He is worried he may lose the captaincy.**

*A   The great thing about the diaphragm is it is a muscle. The more he exercises
it the more he will improve the muscle memory and breathing properly will
become second nature. If he perfects his breath control to raise his voice
he will no longer need to shout in order to be heard. His voice will have
adequate support from his breath control to project to the back of any
playground and beyond. The captain's armband is his to keep if his football
skills keep improving too.*

3

Manners maketh man (and child)

Theatre etiquette means actors understand the importance of listening, when to be quiet and why they must be considerate to others on stage. These are skills children can benefit from enormously.

Isn't it irritating when someone arrives late at the theatre or a mobile phone rings during a performance? Bad manners are bad form.

Some of us would ban virtually every electronic device from theatres, especially personal organisers and alarms on watches. Personally we'd go a step further and send an electrical charge through the seat of anyone arriving after the curtain has risen. Just to teach them a lesson. OK, maybe that's a bit extreme, but adhering to theatre etiquette is crucial if the audience and actors are to enjoy the performance. What we're really talking about here is good old-fashioned politeness. The UK has even held a special Good Manners Day in the past, in which people were encouraged to

Here's an idea for you... **Invite your child to talk on a subject she feels particularly strongly about. Maybe there is an issue between you and your daughter over why she must go to bed at a certain time? Let her talk for two minutes without interruption and then it's your go. It will teach her the skill of listening and appreciating the views of others.**

smile more and to treat others as they would like to be treated. Actually, it would be rude not to take part in such an event.

Your child will gain social skills if she knows when to listen, when to express an opinion and learns not to talk over her friends or interrupt them. She'll learn to be tolerant and accepting of people in society who she might view as different, and this will earn her the respect of her pals and adults.

As in any job, actors are judged by how professional they are, which means knowing how to behave in the theatre. Many a thespian's eyebrow has been raised in recent years at the excruciating antics of reality TV show contestants thrust into the limelight without any idea how to behave on stage or behind it. There are many unwritten rules actors must obey. They must be silent on stage while others act, take on board everyone's ideas during rehearsals, never touch props that don't belong to them and avoid upstaging by hogging the limelight when someone else is reciting their lines.

Getting your child and a friend to stare at each other and talk about the same subject at the same time for 30 seconds is a bit of an eye-opener. When they've finished ask them how much they heard of the other person's comments. It was probably very little. Next, ask them to make up a story by each saying one sentence at a time. By doing this they'll understand the importance of listening, take on board what the other person has said and appreciate why they must be quiet while they say it. Oh, and don't forget to applaud them if the story is good – clapping is another essential part of theatre etiquette and confidence boosting.

Actors are told never to turn their back to the audience, which is more about letting people hear them properly and to see their facial expressions than rudeness, but it is something we can all learn from. Next time you're standing with your back to your child while washing up or working on your computer, think how much better he would feel if he could see your face and emotions as he explains something to you.

Another element of theatre etiquette relevant to your child's life is the importance of good time-keeping. If an actor is not at the theatre half an hour before he's due on stage his understudy will get the part. Similarly, your child does not want to miss out on the best jobs at school or be substitute for his sports team because he arrives late.

Hopefully he'll grow up considering the views of others, which will make him a popular member of his peer group and this will fuel his confidence. It also means he'll avoid any unpleasant shocks when he visits the theatre …!

You cannot beat the feel of a real-life production so make sure you visit one occasionally. IDEA 12, *Ah … the magic of live theatre*, explains just how much you and your child will benefit.

Try another idea…

Associate with well-mannered persons and your manners will improve. Run around with decent folk and your own decent instincts will be strengthened.
STANLEY WALKER, author

Defining idea…

11

Q My daughter has quite good manners but how can I stop her getting so excited when we have friends over for tea? She becomes a real chatterbox and talks over her friends and cousins which irritates them so much they don't want to play with her. What can I do?

A *You need to emphasise to her the importance of listening. Sometimes when we get excited we do start to talk over people. A good drama game to play over dinner is a round of questions. Set out the rules clearly from the start. One question is asked to everyone at the table and each person has 30 seconds to answer it until you move onto the next person. Nobody is allowed to talk at the same time. Try simple questions such as 'What have you been doing today?' or 'What do you like and dislike about our town?' This exercise will highlight to your daughter that she will get her opportunity to speak, but she must be patient and listen to others too.*

Q I am sure my child would enjoy playing a game which helps her to listen but at five isn't she a little young to concentrate when other people are speaking?

A *For younger children you can add further 'rules' to the game to make it even more exciting. Every time somebody talks during another person's 30 seconds they get 'beeped' by the host. This could be you. Oh, the power! If a child gets more than two beeps they miss their go and must wait until the next question.*

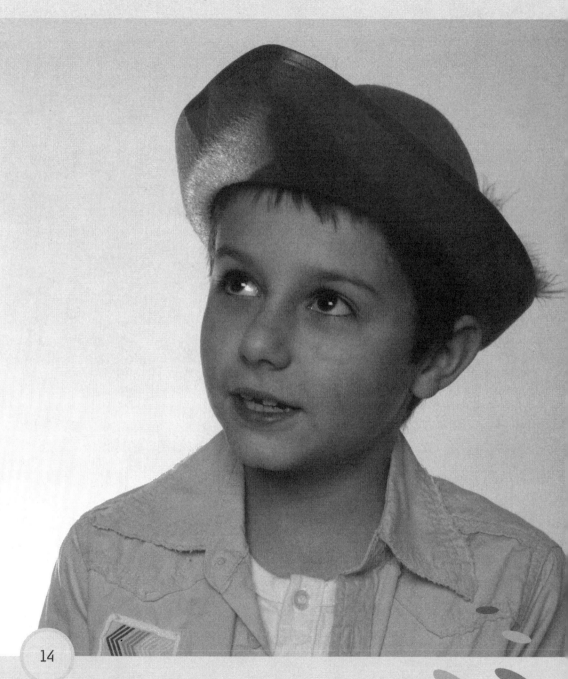

4

Prop till you drop

Don't tell the cleaning police, but clutter is good. Items strewn around the house provide actors with props that add reality to a scene while they can fire a child's imagination.

Never work with children or animals, is the thespian's cry, and one our friend Joanna Forest wishes she'd heeded.

Whilst playing Charlotte in Michael Palin's comedy *The Weekend* in London's West End, Joanna was handed a real life prop to carry – a dog performing the important canine role of Pippa. During one performance the creature jumped out of Jo's arms, left the stage and caused havoc among the startled audience. Props – meaning properties – are essential to any theatre and our homes are stacked full of them. Luckily, most are not breathing and don't need to be walked twice a day. Whether it is Granny's hat, your shoes or an old pair of glasses, any odds and sods hidden away or ready for the dustbin can spark off your child's creative juices, boosting his confidence in the process.

Children love to play shops, mums and dads or hospitals and – let's face it – games become more realistic if they have a broom to sweep with or an old telephone with

Here's an idea for you... **Get your child to sit on a chair and give her a hat. Tell her not to wear it yet but to think about who would wear such a hat. What job would they do and what voice would they have? Maybe add a prop such as a walking stick. Now ask her to put on the hat and talk to you as the person she believes would wear it. It takes the pressure off your child having to be herself, especially if she is shy.**

which to call the doctor. Like an actor, your child wants to make her character as believable as possible. Not just in her mind but in yours too, especially as you will probably be asked to join in at some point. Come on, you know you want to!

Actors spend hours practising using props. It is harder than you might think to do simple tasks such as opening or shutting a door or pouring a drink whilst reciting lines and interacting with others on stage. Some actors complain that using props compromises their artistic licence. Luckily this is one grumble you are unlikely to hear from your child. Props are fun and there are plenty of games to play that will boost your child's self-esteem. A great one is to give him and his friends an item like a hairbrush and tell them to pretend it is something different. First they must imagine it is a microphone and next a posh pen to write with. Or try this. Hand them three props and tell them to go away and come back with a story to act out using those items. If you also persuade them to write a script then – hey presto! – before you know it you'll have a free performance on your hands. You'll be amazed by the kind of things children will come up with and how pleased they will be with what they've achieved.

Many items make good props but adding a costume really brings things to life so visit IDEA 11, *Dressing the part, make-up and all*, for some more tips.

Try another idea…

As children get older and start school, props can be used to take their minds off a problem and help them to discuss it with you. You can get a lot of information out of someone whilst sharing a pretend cup of tea in a make-believe café, even if the tiny table and chairs are not the most comfortable. If you don't have suitable props at home they are easy to find. One man's junk is another man's treasure, and charity shops, boot fairs and relatives' attics can be goldmines. If you are a clutter-worrier then create a Prop Box which can be stored in your child's bedroom or in a spare room. You may like to help your child create his own props using arts and crafts materials. Making props for a puppet show can certainly help shy children come out of themselves as they tend to speak more loudly and clearly when talking as a marionette. There is another benefit from using everyday items as props in games. It can reduce the amount of money you have to spend on new toys that hardly ever get played with. Now there's a thought.

'Man is a tool-using animal. Without tools he is nothing, with tools he is all.'
THOMAS CARLYLE, Scottish historian

Defining idea…

17

How did it go?

Q   **I am a single parent living in a one-bedroom flat with two children and I don't have room for lots of bits and pieces that may be played with only occasionally. How can my children enjoy props?**

A   *Props do not have to be large. One tip is to condense items into one small box that will fit on top of a wardrobe or under a bed. Put small items into it, such as an old mobile phone rather than a broken landline phone, spectacles rather than a hat and a toy teapot instead of a complete tea set.*

Q   **Won't it take away some of the excitement if the props available to my child are limited in such a way?**

A   *Not at all. Many props can double up as different things. A small notebook is also a passport or a traffic warden's ticket book. You can also keep some paper, card and colouring pencils in the box to make new props as you go along.*

5

How Now Brown Cow

No one expects your child to sound like a 1940s BBC public service broadcast, but if he can express himself confidently people will listen to what he has to say.

A few years ago the novelist Beryl Bainbridge suggested all children should have elocution lessons to wipe out their regional accents.

Strangely Ms Bainbridge, a former actress, did not originally speak with a traditional BBC voice herself. She was born in Liverpool in the 1930s and had elocution lessons from the age of 11 to remove her Liverpudlian dialect. Some people would argue that taking such a radical step was completely unnecessary. After all, a Liverpool drawl did not do the Beatles any harm. From a very early age our voice is our most basic communication tool. Thankfully, where children live and how they sound is now far less important than whether they can talk clearly, expressively and with energy. If your child can speak without mumbling she will be more articulate and confident in the classroom or when playing with friends. It should also mean she removes any irritating lazy speaking habits such as replacing 'th' with 'f' or dropping her 'h's'. ''Ow foroughly 'orrible.'

Here's an idea for you...

There is a game called I'm Here Great Master, which makes children aware of their voices and how they can change and disguise it. Get one friend to sit on a chair with their back to the others. A child says 'I'm Here Great Master' in a voice or accent different to their own and the child on the chair must guess who said it.

To an actor, the voice is crucial (unless he is a mime artist, of course). A performer must be able to deliver lines with an accent if required and at the correct speed to suit the text and his character's personality. His words must also be well-projected so everyone in the audience can hear him. The actors' vocal warm-up before a show is a joy to behold. Try blagging your way backstage one day and you'll probably see the cast reciting the alphabet, singing really fast songs or exercising their jaws by pretending to chew a toffee. Don't be surprised if you spot the leading lady with her tongue hanging out as she reels off the months of the year backwards.

Tongue twisters are great for helping your child practise her speaking. There are well-known favourites such as 'Unique New York' but it is more fun if you can create your own.

Speech and breathing go together like gin and tonic – so flick through IDEA 2, *The ins and outs of breathing*, when you have time.

Try another idea…

Here are a couple of silly ones we thought up in less than a minute:

Really red robins run riot

Or how about:

Lazy Lou lost little Lilly's lavender locket

The tongue's role in our lives goes way beyond being the primary bodily organ for taste. Where it is placed in our mouth determines how every sound we make is uttered. Try a 'llll' sound and then a 'rrrr' and notice how your tongue is in a different place each time. The famous phrase 'How Now Brown Cow' comes from a 19th century nursery rhyme and is used by speech experts to give children and adults more rounded vowel sounds. Have you ever heard your own voice, maybe on a holiday or wedding video? It can be excruciatingly embarrassing because nobody sounds how they think they do. Children are no exception. Teaching your child to speak with upward and downward inflections and to open his mouth wider when talking will help him develop a clear and expressive voice rather than sounding monotone. Actors call this adding light and shade to their voice. If

'Talk low, talk slow, and don't talk too much.'

JOHN WAYNE

Defining idea…

Defining idea...

'Make sure you have finished speaking before your audience has finished listening.'

DOROTHY SARNOFF, speech and image consultant

your child's voice sounds interesting and she speaks at the right pace, other people will want to listen to her and this will give her the confidence to contribute during group conversations.

One way to help your child is to record him reading a boring shopping list and then letting him hear how he sounds. Then record him reading a passage from a book or magazine in the style of a newsreader, then as a children's television presenter or in a posh voice followed by an American accent. He will soon notice how different and appealing his own voice can sound.

Whoever said children should be seen and not heard?

Q   **My daughter talks to her friends in some kind of street talk and I don't want her talking that way to adults. Am I wasting my time trying to change her?**

How did it go?

A   *There are always trends in speech as we grow up, but it is important your daughter can distinguish how she talks to her friends with how she speaks to her family and other adults. Why not try a game where you all pretend to have dinner as a posh family one night to see if she can avoid street talk? Be careful, though, because you will irritate her if you keep picking her up on her speech and she might become reluctant to talk to you at all.*

Q   **If she thinks we want her to talk as a posh person, won't she be going from one extreme to the other?**

A   *Of course you don't want her to speak like the Queen, but by taking speech to the limits it is easy to bring different tones down or up a few notches. This type of exercise will make your child realise how people view her by how the talks and how she sounds. There is always room in life for your child to talk differently depending on who she is with and she will be more confident in all situations if she can make distinctions.*

6

Thanks for the memory

Actors must be able to memorise lines, and children who can retain information learn faster and are less likely to make embarrassing mistakes.

We knew a biology teacher once who made her pupils memorise whole chapters from their books and recite chunks of text at the end of the lesson.

The children hated her, but they learned quickly under pressure and remembered facts. One friend who suffered at the hands of Biology Barbara can still reel off parrot-fashion the definition of photosynthesis to anyone who cares to listen. A strong memory is a valuable skill. Your child will feel confident if she can answer her teacher's questions and has memorised the heel/toe/heel/toe steps in her Tuesday dance class. Revising for exams should also be less daunting as she grows up and she will hopefully avoid those little social gaffes and toe-curling experiences we've all suffered, such as forgetting a person's name when we meet them.

An actor without a good memory is like a mechanic trying to blow up a car tyre with a bike pump. He can still do the job but it is much easier if he has the right

Here's an idea for you... **Find a child-friendly magazine and choose a short article such as a film review. Get your child to read through the story a couple of times and then ask him to tell you in his own words what the article was about. You'll be amazed how closely he will reproduce what he has just read. Children often find it easier than adults to memorise information quickly. Swap places and see the look of satisfaction on his face when he realises his memory is better than yours.**

tools. In fact, an actor will struggle to develop a character's personality until he knows his lines off by heart. Many children have problems remembering information. A poor memory and forgetfulness in youngsters is often blamed on distractions such as television and computer games, and it is true this whole area does relate to concentration and being able to listen. When an actor forgets his words it is often because he has something on his mind. William Shakespeare was well aware of the memory flaws in some of his actors. Apparently it was the main reason he wrote his plays in the regular rhythm known as blank verse. He needed them to learn their lines fast, often in less than a week. Paul Nicholas, who has appeared in British sitcoms and West End stage shows, tells us he locks himself in a room, records the whole script onto a tape recorder and presses the pause button on his lines to help him memorise his words quickly. Actors will also use recall games to keep their memories in trim and kids can use them too.

The old favourite in our house is 'I went to the supermarket and I bought ...', where children each add one item whilst remembering what other people bought and in what order. This can be made easier for younger children by using the alphabet, although you may find they buy a lot of Apples, Bananas and Cakes. You get the gist.

Another game involves putting ten items on a table, letting your child look at them for a couple of minutes, then asking her to turn her back whilst you remove one object. Can she guess what is missing? Many children struggle to remember the spelling of certain words so one tip is to try making up a sentence using all the letters. Take the word 'occasion' where children always forget how many 'c's' and 's's' there are. She might, however, be able to remember Ostriches Catch Colds And Sneeze In Orange Napkins. She could learn a funny action to help her remember the phrase.

If she is nervous about a school assembly or her role as Mary in the school nativity play, try rehearsing her lines over and over again. If she reads the other parts as well, she will become familiar with the whole script and remember when exactly she needs to usher in little Jimmy, James and Joshua who are playing the three wise men but keep messing about at the side of the stage. Kids learn so much from listening and observing that you might be surprised by how quickly your child develops a good memory and how her confidence grows.

Oh yes, in case you were wondering, photosynthesis is the process by which a plant makes food for itself. Now don't you forget it!

Reading poetry is a great way to help kids improve their memory. Glance at IDEA 13, *Once upon a time, a man made up a rhyme*, for some inspiration.

Try another idea…

'Memory is the diary that we all carry about with us.'
OSCAR WILDE

Defining idea…

How did it go?

Q **Word association games have helped my daughter become more confident in her spelling, but how can I get her to feel more positive about her times tables in numeracy?**

A *Actors often remember important lines by associating what they need to learn with a song. This technique works with numbers too. Try singing the four times table to the tune of 'Knees Up Mother Brown' or 'Happy Birthday' and the figures will soon stick in her head. It is a canny technique used by car insurance advertisers to get us to remember phone numbers on television and radio commercials.*

Q **But won't her teacher find it odd if she sings in class?**

A *Her singing may be quite entertaining but you are probably right. However, by practising the songs at home, the information will stay in her mind and she should be able to recite her tables without having to sing out loud. There are other health benefits to singing too, of course. Therapists in New York have found that banging out a song from time to time decreases blood pressure and reduces stress. This is something for you to mention the next time the neighbours complain about your singing in the shower. You might also discover that your daughter has a passion for singing and wants to join the school choir.*

7

Lovely darling, but ...

In the same way that theatre critics can hit a raw nerve, children can be very sensitive to criticism. Yet constructive comments can encourage them to try harder.

Here's a tip for you. The best night to get tickets for the theatre is Press Night when the actors try just that little bit harder to impress the critics.

Some actors will tell you they never read reviews, whilst others wait until their final show before taking a peep at the journalists' comments, scared their own self-confidence will be shattered if they look beforehand. The truth is most actors have egos as fragile as an ancient Ming vase and dread anyone criticising their work, especially if the remarks are rude and personal. The best actors take the good with the bad and develop a skin as hard as a rhino hide.

It is not only theatre critics who voice an opinion. A director will dissect every performance and it's never a good career move to argue. Actors must accept any observations and use them to their advantage. After all, if their critics are right they will get a longer round of applause the next time they perform. Children need to realise criticism will fly their way occasionally and that it can knock their confidence. Your

Here's an idea for you...
By getting your child to elaborate on his answers he will learn to be constructive in his criticism. After a family day out, sit down with him and produce an objective critique of what went on. What were the good and bad points of the day and why? What could have been more fun and what would he have done differently if he'd been in charge of organising everything?

child must learn to channel any criticism positively so he understands why sometimes he needs to try that little bit harder.

When some dance teachers are preparing students for exams, they'll give a child a score of 100% before they begin a routine and take off marks for each mistake. The dancer is pleased to end up with a score of around 90% but realises she can improve. In our house, this idea works well if there is a list of jobs that our son or daughter needs to do, such as tidy their room or do their homework. They start with 100% and are told they will get a better reward the higher their score is at the end of the day.

Children, like actors, love to be praised. We are not talking about some ancient Chinese therapy of ego massage here, but balancing a negative comment aimed at your child with a positive one. Constructive criticism in life, as in the theatre, should be a way of offering credible advice. During rehearsals for a stage production a good director will:

■ Never do an impression of the actor when criticising her.
■ Always mention positive points about her performance before remarking on something he didn't like.
■ Make suggestions of how the actor can improve – and give her more time to get things right.

The trick is to highlight what you're looking for from your child. For instance, if you think a family photo session at the local photographers might be quite stressful (I know, how *do* you keep a six-year-old's hair looking nice long enough to get that cute snap?) give your child three goals to achieve. These might be to sit still, not fidget and to smile.

Directors have the power in the theatre and children can learn a lot from directing their own lives and learning from their mistakes. See IDEA 17, *Don't argue with the director.*

Try another idea...

If he doesn't do all these things straightaway, don't get anxious and criticise him for the things he didn't manage but congratulate him on what he did achieve. Say how impressed you would be if he could now smile more because Granny really wants to see that big grin with his two front teeth missing.

It is a reality of life that children can be cruel to one another and are sometimes overly critical. It is also the case that children often find it easier to say something negative about their own personality than something positive. When your child has some friends over, get them each to say two nice things about their pals and see the happy reaction. It will help your son to appreciate his own good points if others point them out.

'Sandwich every bit of criticism between two thick layers of praise.'
MARY KAY ASH, businesswoman

Defining idea...

Children are better than adults at picking up on their own flaws. That's one criticism parents must just take on the chin and learn from.

'No matter who says what, you should accept it with a smile and do your own work.'
MOTHER TERESA

Defining idea...

How did it go?

Q   **My daughter is very self-critical and worries she is not as good at some things as her friends. How do I get her to believe in herself?**

A   *Remind her of the things she is good at and the things she is better at than her friends. Encourage her to try new things by showing her you have 100% belief that she can do it, and reward her when she makes positive progress. Don't push her too far and criticise her mistakes, because children do excel at different things. Many actors are better at playing some parts than others, such as princesses or villains, and need support if they step out of their comfort zone.*

Q   **Unfortunately many of my daughter's friends attend the same after-school clubs and she is not confident enough to go to new clubs on her own. What can I do about this?**

A   *There are so many different activities kids can try these days, from something as extreme as rock-climbing to hula-hooping. Work with her to find something she would really enjoy. Let her choose what excites her from a list of clubs in your area so she is more confident about attending. Drama classes are particularly good for making new friends because there are a lot of team activities where everyone contributes different skills.*

8

Looking the part is part of the look

Knowing how to present ourselves in a confident manner becomes vital as we get older. You can help your child to sit up straight, make eye-contact and improve his overall posture.

Those strange body language experts appearing on the sofas during daytime TV claim more than 90% of how we communicate is non-verbal. Apparently words are purely the building blocks during any tête-à-tête.

Fidgeting, picking our nails or avoiding someone's gaze displays a complete lack of confidence and insecurity, whilst a brisk walk into a room oozes self-assurance. It seems that even when we are not speaking we are still giving out signals. Next time

Here's an idea for you... **Your child needs to know that first impressions count. Ask her and a group of friends to try to remember the first time they saw each other. Do they remember what they were all wearing or what they said? They can go through all their various classmates, including the teachers and discuss first impressions and whether they were right or wrong.**

you are enduring a gruelling job interview remember not to cross your arms and legs – even if you do need the toilet – as this is a very defensive gesture.

Children tend to slouch with hunched shoulders, play with their hair or jiggle their legs when they're nervous. If your child can look confident by the way she stands, sits and moves, she will feel bolder because of the positive way others react to her.

An actor must be aware of everything his body does on stage. He needs to strip away his own personal mannerisms and establish new ones when building a character. Actors spend ages getting their posture just right and your child will appear more confident if she can too. This may sound like some weird yoga exercise but stay with us. Ideally her weight should be evenly distributed over the balls of her feet, with her shoulders relaxed and her chin at right angles to the neck. She can find this position by leaning forward so she is almost touching the floor and then swinging her arms from side to side. If she rises up slowly to the standing position she will feel her whole body coming to an aligned central position.

Practice makes perfect when learning how to present yourself confidently so have a look at IDEA 1, *Who says life's not a rehearsal?*

Try another idea…

There are also some wonderful acting techniques to help younger children stand still.

- Actors must often be motionless on stage so they practise by playing the run and freeze game. Most children have itchy feet, so getting them to stop and start will build up a tolerance for standing and sitting without moving. Such a skill might help them get chosen for the best jobs in class.
- Sleeping Lions is an old classic. Most children in a group are lions and two are hunters. The lions pretend to be asleep and the hunters must wake them without touching them. They can go close to their prey and even tell them awful jokes to make them giggle. Where do lions live? On the *mane* road.

How confidently children walk can certainly affect how they are viewed by other people. When they swagger they can come across as aggressive, so it is certainly not advisable to walk into the head teacher's office strutting like the Artful Dodger from *Oliver Twist.*

'Courage is what it takes to stand up and speak; courage is also what it takes to sit down and listen.'
WINSTON CHURCHILL

Defining idea…

Here's a quick walking exercise to help your child become more aware of how he moves.

Ask him to stroll around the room looking nervous and shifty like a prospective shoplifter. Then get him to stride as a snobby rich person and then as a cool teenager wearing headphones listening to music. Your child will notice how people can make a snap judgement about someone simply by how they walk. Does it make them look trustworthy or dishonest?

If you have younger children you could learn this poem together and play a little game.

I'm a prince (or princess)
I'm an elf
I'm a teddy sitting on a shelf
I am a soldier
I'm a bee
But best of all I am me.

When you call out the name of each character your child must react to how they think each character would move. They might curtsy like a princess, be cheeky like an elf, stand tall as a soldier, slump as a teddy bear or run around buzzing like a bee. You could have a turn too if you like.

Q When I pointed out to my daughter that she chewed her hair when she was nervous and it was distracting to others, she stopped. However, when I told my son he was always scuffing the floor with his feet when trying to stand still, he became very self-conscious about it and seems to have lost some confidence. How can I repair the damage?

How did it go?

A *The best thing you can do is not mention it again, although you still want him to stop scuffing his shoes. Try playing a game that does not seem to relate to the problem. There is Guess What Statue I Am, where he must stand like a soldier, a superhero or a baddy, and you must guess who he is. Then make his character stand like a king. There is no need to mention his feet again. In fact, it is never a good idea to directly point out negatives in your child.*

Q How can I be sure he will associate this game with standing still in his class assemblies? When I am watching he seems to be the only one fidgeting and looking really uncomfortable.

A *Once he has mastered standing correctly in character poses, the next time he is delivering his lines in the class assembly, tell him he looks his best standing still like the king. He should find this advice easier to relate to than continually being told to keep his feet still.*

9
Games, sets and matchsticks

Not every child excels academically and, like great set designers in the theatre, it can be through their creative talents that their self-esteem soars.

Behind every great company of actors is a fantastically gifted team of set designers who bring a show to life.

Think back to your first visit to the theatre and what really excited you. For me it was seeing Sleeping Beauty's castle on stage whilst waiting for the Christmas pantomime to begin in our dilapidated village hall. No-one was pretending it was London's West End – in fact, thinking about it, the turrets were rather tatty – but the scenery was still an essential part of telling the story. Whatever the standard of the production, the set helps the actors become their characters and the audience to understand exactly what's happening. While the performer uses words and movement to create the perfect atmosphere, the set designer is a dab hand with carpentry and painting.

Set designers are basically adults who are very good at arts and crafts. If your child has flair in this direction (maybe she is a whiz at junk modelling in the classroom) it could be the best route to improving her confidence. Her talents will impress her teachers, friends and, obviously, her family. Set designers are paid well in the thea-

Here's an idea for you... **Next time you're planning a family gathering make sure you have plenty of art and craft materials in the house. Most children love to put on a production, so work out beforehand the theme of the show you want them to produce for the adults and get the kids to design a basic set with props. You'll find that the children who do not want to be one of the performers will still enjoy taking part, either making the sets or bringing them on 'stage' when needed. Maybe they could make and hold cardboard clouds to create the impression of wizards flying?**

tre because their efforts can help to disguise a poor script or disappointing acting. Children who hate being the centre of attention or are maybe not as outgoing as their brothers or sisters can flourish as the creative brains that improve the games they play together.

London theatre set creator Sadie Cook tells us the best scenery comes from exploring your imagination and taking clues from the script. 'One story about a journalist used a set totally covered in newspaper which we put up using wallpaper paste and covered in varnish to stop the print rubbing off on the actors,' she says. 'There was also a bedroom scene with a window, behind which we painted skyscrapers to make it look like New York.' Sadie works closely with the director to sketch out ideas and keeps a scrapbook of every project which is her inspiration in the future. Keeping an ideas folder at home can generate those essential light-bulb-above-the-head moments when you and your child are staring at a blank piece of paper.

If you are finding it hard to come up with ideas, get your child to make something related to her favourite story. Maybe she loves mermaids and could make a rock and then the sea and paint it blue? She can then play a game involving her favourite toys using the 'set' she has made herself.

Here's another idea. Next time you have a Halloween or Christmas party, ask your child to create decorations to display around the house or to place on the table. He'll receive positive comments from those attending.

There is a saying that good art is in the eye of the beholder, and there is no right or wrong way a stage set should look. A designer might give a modern feel to an old story or set a contemporary play in an ancient castle. In fact, the sky's the limit where artistic panache is concerned, which is something to reinforce when your child is busy creating her own masterpiece.

Making puppets is a great way to boost the confidence of shy children. They can make cardboard characters and scenery, colour in everything and put on a show. Nervous children are often more confident producing voices from behind a screen. Similarly, producing character masks can help to get your child speaking more boldly.

Children's confidence grows when they're having fun and there are few things more entertaining for kids than making an arty mess and having something they can proudly say they made themselves. It's time to get your hands dirty.

An actor's props go hand in hand with set design so take a peep at IDEA 4, *Prop till you drop*, for ideas on how to add even more fire to your child's imagination.

Try another idea...

'Painting is the most beautiful of all arts. In it, all sensations are condensed; contemplating it, everyone can create a story at the will of his imagination.'
PAUL GAUGUIN, artist

Defining idea...

How did
it go? **Q** **My husband and I are not very artistic and we work long hours. How can we meet the demands of the school for our daughter to make objects for the many theme weeks her class enjoys?**

A *Your child should be doing all the hard work here. Your role is to ensure she has the right tools for the job by making sure there are arts and craft items in the home and she can find them easily. Although it may seem like it sometimes, schools are not creating art competitions for parents. The teacher wants your child, however old she is, to display her own creativity and she will be rewarded for it.*

Q **That's all very well but her class are reading *The Lion, the Witch and the Wardrobe* and she has volunteered to make a miniature wardrobe to bring in to school to assist with the telling of the story. Help?**

A *Don't panic. In the theatre, some of the best sets are the most simple. To create a great wardrobe get a cardboard box and paint it brown. Then your artistic skills do not have to stretch any further than painting a line down the middle and a door knob on either side. Simple, but it will still look great.*

10

We should always trust our instincts

Trust can take ages to earn but only seconds to lose. Actors must trust each other implicitly on stage, while children always think carefully about who they can rely on.

It was the Scottish author and poet George MacDonald who wowed his friends with the words that to be trusted is a greater compliment than to be loved.

Actors need to trust one another on stage and be confident that if one of them forgets their lines another will cover up any possible embarrassment. If a performer is lifted up or carried in a scene she needs to know she won't be dropped and break her ankle. Of course, her jealous understudy might not share such concerns for her safety.

Children decide quickly whether they can put their faith in someone. We all want our kids to be streetwise but we also want them to trust responsible adults.

It can become a problem if a child is too scared to go home from school with a friend's mum or too nervous to visit the hospital or the hairdresser. Billy the barber may be a lovely old man full of shearing anecdotes to you, but to your son he's just a strange man brandishing a dangerous pair of scissors.

In the theatre the rehearsal process is all about building up trust. An actress playing the girlfriend of a male actor she has never met before will need some ice-breaking exercises to remove any awkwardness. The director will often ask the actors to massage one another's shoulders on the first day or talk about a very personal experience.

If your child has trouble trusting others then getting him to share private information can help. You might need him to trust other family members or one of your friends so ask them to chat to your son. They could talk about what he wants to do when he grows up and whether he would like to have his own children one day. This sharing of personal 'secrets' will help him relax.

Here's an idea for you... **Ask your child to stand in the biggest room in your house. Place obstacles on the floor, such as books, boxes or toys and then blindfold her. It is your job to direct her to the other side of the room using directions such as 'go left' or 'straight ahead'. Once she has successfully made it across, swap roles so she learns how other people will sometimes put their trust in her.**

Role playing is a great way to build up a child's trust in adults who are there to help him, such as his friends' parents or the family doctor or dentist.

Set up a game where your child is the doctor and his brother or sister is the patient. You effectively direct the scene by telling your son to explain why he needs to look at the patient's leg. Games like this encourage physical contact in a controlled environment. The kids can even dress up and make their own doctor's kit, including tissues for bandages and brooms turned upside down for crutches.

We've all been in that situation where our child is too shy to play with the child of an adult friend who is visiting. One fun drama game you can try here is to sit the children together and, with your help, ask them to try and discover three things that the other child likes and one he hates.

Friends need to trust each other as they are often working together so read through IDEA 44, *That's what friends are for*, front and backstage.

Try another idea…

By sharing such personal information your son may discover this other child, Kevin, who he thought was incredibly dull, also detests Brussels sprouts and likes playing pirates. It is on such simple common ground that lifetime friendships are built.

As your child learns to trust others he'll also find it easier to develop dependable relationships with adults other than his parents. It is important he has the confidence to turn to one of your friends or another trustworthy grown-up at school other than his teacher. One tip is to find an adult who shares a common interest with your child, such as football, cars or dancing, who can act as a mentor vetted by you.

'A great partnership requires an equal degree of trust. One must trust the other yet one must also trust oneself.'
SARAH LAMB, principle dancer with
The Royal Ballet

Defining idea…

Also remember it can be hard for children to learn to trust others if their parents are sometimes negative towards people simply because of the way they look or behave.

How did it go?

Q   **My child thinks I'm going to leave her at the parent and toddler group. How can I stop her clinging to me throughout the session so I can enjoy some adult company?**

A   *This has to be a gradual process. Take the initiative by starting an ice-breaking game. One slightly silly exercise used by actors when they first meet is called Duck Duck Goose. Get all the parents and children to sit in a circle. A child plays the role of 'duck' and walks around the circle touching the heads of the others and saying 'duck' each time. Eventually they call 'goose' when they touch someone's head. The goose must chase the duck around the circle until the duck makes it to the goose's space and sits down. Then the goose becomes the duck and the game is repeated. This will get your child sitting in different places alongside children they wouldn't automatically choose to be next to. Your daughter may only watch to start with but will soon want to join in.*

Q   **Is it really my place to suggest a game at the parent and toddler group?**

A   *The subject of trust extends to adults. You need to be confident enough to be assertive and make suggestions and trust that others will not dismiss your idea. You must trust your judgement because you know your idea will help the children. Your child's confidence will also grow because she'll be proud that Mum or Dad has suggested a game.*

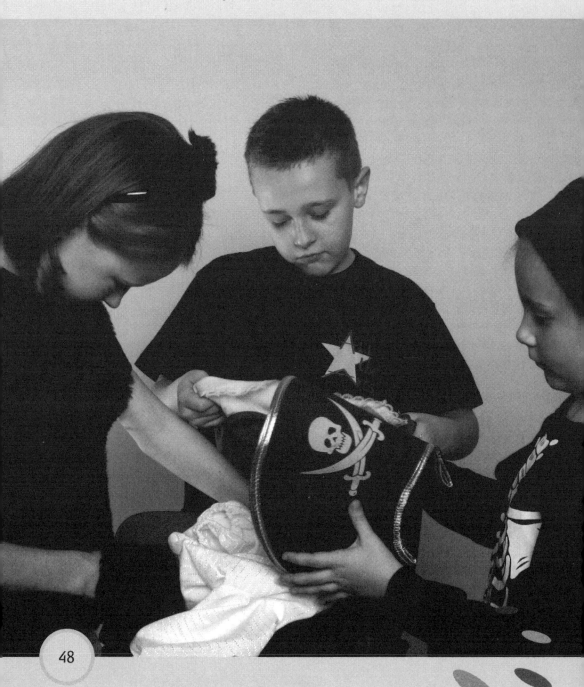

11
Dressing the part, make-up and all

Actors love putting on costumes and children adore dressing up and having their faces painted. Watch your child become more adventurous as he transforms himself into a superhero for a few hours.

In Elizabethan theatre women were banned from the stage, so adolescent boys played female characters and wore elaborate costumes to add that touch of reality.

More than 300 years later costumes remain an integral part of any theatre production and squeezing into bodices and corsets is now – usually – left to the ladies. OK, we know, British pantomime is the weird exception which proves the rule. Oh yes it is! Costumes help the audience to understand a scene's historical setting, a character's social class and whether they should feel sympathy or disdain for someone on stage. Most actors are convinced they cannot really embrace a role until they're wearing the correct attire. This all makes sense if you think about it. An actor playing a witch should feel more at home in a black hat, cloak and hobnail boots, whilst

Here's an idea for you... **If your family is planning a trip to the theatre or to an event like a Wild West Show, see if you and your child can create a costume that will enhance his experience. If he's dressed up he may have the confidence to volunteer to go on stage and his self-esteem will be lifted by the positive comments he'll receive about his costume throughout the day.**

the role of a librarian will come easier to an actor once her hair is tied back and she's wearing glasses. Yes, these are awful stereotypes so slap us now, but that's the main ingredient for many great characterisations.

Put children in a room with a box of dressing-up clothes and they'll soon be fighting over who should wear the fairy outfit, dress up as the superhero or the nurse. Costumes will fuel your child's imagination and give her the confidence to explore her emotions and interact with other kids. These outfits are disguises behind which less secure children can lose their inhibitions.

There is a simple game to illustrate this. Ask two children to put on different costumes. One can be a shopkeeper and the other a mum visiting the store. You will find that because your child knows from his own experience what a shop assistant and his mum would say over the counter, he's not short of words and will throw himself into the scene. There are other familiar storylines you can use too, such as going to the doctor or the school teacher and pupil scenario.

Yes, we know the price of kids' costumes in the high street can be expensive – but you don't have to spend a fortune. Take a look around the house. That stripy T-shirt that no longer fits you (come on, admit it) is crying out to be a burglar's outfit supported by a big swag bag. And don't you think it would be much better to turn that old pillow case into a ghost costume rather than another duster?

One tip is to keep all the costumes you make in a box so your child can use them time and again for those many themed birthday parties she's bound to be invited to. It'll stop both of you worrying about creating something new every time and old costumes can always be improved with some creative accessories.

Dressing up is an ideal way to reassure a nervous child worried about a particular event. If he is dreading a trip to the dentist, why not let him dress as a pirate while having his teeth checked? It will certainly lighten the mood at the surgery, but he might have to lose the parrot.

And don't forget the importance of make-up in this bizarre world of dressing-up.

Actors practise for hours to get their look absolutely right so they don't appear washed out when the theatre lights shine down on them. Of course, that would have been the least of the actors' worries in Shakespeare's time when performers covered their faces in highly-poisonous lead-based make-up which caused many a health calamity.

If your child likes having her face painted get her and a friend to decorate each other's faces. She might discover she is really creative and will get a real buzz from discovering something else she's good at.

Costumes come alive if props are added. Take a look at the gems scattered around your house in IDEA 4, *Prop till you drop.*

Try another idea…

'I'm like an eight-year-old with a dressing up box. I have the luxury of being able to change on a whim.'
KYLIE MINOGUE

Defining idea…

How did it go?

Q   We have a dressing-up box in our house for our four-year-old son and daughter, who are twins. My son always wants to dress up as the fairy so how can we persuade him to wear the cowboy or the doctor's outfit instead?

A   *The important thing at this age is that your child is expressing himself through dressing up. The lovely thing about kids is they haven't got the same hang-ups as their parents. In the theatre some of the butchest looking men will wear frocks occasionally. Think of the characters in the many Christmas shows across the world each year. By making an issue out of your son's choice of outfit you risk putting him off dressing up altogether.*

Q   One mum in our street is a whiz with a needle and thread and I always feel under pressure. We've tried making our own costumes but they don't look very good to me. Any tips on making homemade costumes more impressive?

A   *The standard of the costume is not as important as how your child feels when he's wearing it and the imaginative ideas it helps him develop. Children also have a more vivid imagination than grown-ups. They are more than capable of playing the prince in the school play wearing nothing more than a gold-coloured cardboard crown. This is not about spending time and money trying to create something which would not look out of place in London's West End or on Broadway.*

12

Ah ... the magic of live theatre

Your child's listening and observation skills will improve with regular visits to the theatre. If she can grasp information quickly, she'll have the confidence to lead from the front.

The atmosphere's electric, you can almost touch the actors and there is that reassuring smell of freshly painted scenery. So turn off the TV and get some tickets to a real-life production.

It is a sad state of affairs that many children only go to the theatre once a year to see their local Christmas show where they are encouraged to cheer the prince, adore the princess and boo the baddie. There's nothing wrong with that, of course. In fact, we all enjoy shouting at the stage from time to time. What's disturbing is that mums and dads don't see the enjoyment on their little angels' faces as a sign that, perhaps, they should walk through a theatre's doors more often. If your child gets

Here's an idea for you... **If you have a theatre trip planned, get your child to research the story like an actor would research her character. She could surf the internet or visit the library to discover the roots of the plot. After seeing the show she can write a pretend review for a newspaper. This activity will give her the confidence to contribute when her teacher asks who did something interesting at the weekend.**

used to listening and observing live theatre she'll become more perceptive, her attention span will increase and her concentration levels will improve. And that's not all. As she gets better at all of these things her verbal and non-verbal skills, such as her reading, will develop. At school she'll get a confidence boost when the teacher praises her for remembering instructions the first time while her classmates are waiting for commands to be repeated because they weren't listening quite so intently.

We're not suggesting you should drag your seven-year-old to a high-brow performance of Shakespeare's *The Taming of the Shrew*. But you could consider the many children's theatre companies touring the country. Or how about going to a professional musical such as *The Lion King*? She'll love it. Even shows put on by your local amateur drama group can be surprisingly entertaining and are usually very family-friendly. When younger children visit the theatre they often come away wanting to be a dancer or to dress up like the pretty princess. In fact, a visit to a stage show can give them the confidence to join a drama club, dancing school or to learn an instrument, which will boost their self-esteem and could possibly change their life. If a performer asks for volunteers your daughter will see what fun the children on stage are having. She will want the admiration and appreciation those kids felt as they were applauded for taking part. It could mean that next time you visit a show she'll be more inclined to put her nerves aside and might surprise you by raising her hand.

You can make the most of the whole theatre experience by:

- Buying seats near the front so your child can see everything that's going on
- Checking the production is appropriate for your child's age. If you think it might be a bit complicated, explain the plot beforehand so he does not spend the entire first act asking questions to the annoyance of those around you. A short explanation before you arrive can also help to build up the excitement.

He'll also learn the importance of sitting still and being quiet when he attends a public performance. This is a skill many adults haven't even mastered. Odd as it may seem, some people still confuse going to the theatre with visiting the cinema or watching television. They'll mutter away during a show, not realising the actors can often hear every word.

One actress friend remembers a scene when she had to kiss the leading man. Her concentration was broken when she overheard a conversation between two old women in the front row. 'Don't they make a lovely couple, go on kiss him,' one whispered rather loudly to her friend. The moment was almost lost.

Nothing more to say really, apart from look, listen, enjoy and most importantly – come back to the theatre again soon.

There are rules actors and the audience must follow during any show so check out IDEA 3, *Manners maketh man (and child)*, all about theatre etiquette.

Try another idea...

'Seeing a live performance is a stunning experience for kids. The excitement heightens their perceptions and little things are noticed as a whole world of wonder opens up. After taking a bunch of kids to a show I asked one girl "What did you think?" "I'm still getting my chin off the floor," she replied.'

Defining idea...

PETER LATHAN,
Editor of the *British Theatre Guide*

55

How did
it go? **Q** **I am not disputing the benefit of children visiting the theatre but how can I justify the cost of tickets when I have three kids?**

A *The cost of going to the theatre can seem prohibitive and is a reason why families don't go more often. With a bit of research it's possible to unearth some really good shows locally. Many amateur groups put on good productions and charge just a few pounds for tickets. Most companies are also desperate for help behind the scenes making scenery and costumes so if you offer your services you might get a few tickets for free.*

Q **I know what you mean. Our local theatre group is always getting great reviews in the paper and our neighbours never miss a show. But we'd really like to see a professional performance, so what's the best way to make this affordable?**

A *If you really want to see shows in the big city, go during the previews. Check out some theatre ticket websites or contact the venues directly to discover when these are taking place. You could always take a chance and turn up at a theatre at the last minute and hope for some spare tickets but you risk being disappointed. There is also plenty of fringe theatre taking place, often starring television actors trying to break into theatre.*

13

Once upon a time, a man made up a rhyme

Forget Shakespeare's sonnets – children's poetry should be silly, fun and perfect for getting kids to read aloud and explore their feelings through words. It can also help improve their memory.

Alongside flashy computer games poems can seem rather old fashioned. Not so. If the verses are about teachers being aliens, kissing hairy aunties or breaking wind, kids will love them.

What's great about poetry is that it has no rules. Poems can be long or short and they don't even have to rhyme – although young children tend to prefer them if they do and if they have an enjoyable, musical rhythm. Actors learn poetry to develop variations in their voice and alter their pace and pitch. This is a useful trick to have when performing a radio play where facial expressions are redundant and you must rely solely on the tone of your voice to ensure the audience connects with

Here's an
idea for
you…

If there is a big family birthday approaching, ask your child to compose a special poem for that person. It could be funny or heartfelt and included with a birthday card. If he is feeling really brave he could give a rendition of the poem at the party. This is not about creating the best poem in the world but seeing the recipient chuffed to bits and your child receiving lots of praise for his efforts.

your character. The length and structure of poems helps actors develop their breathing because they know they must take a breath at the end of each line. Poetry is a great way to get your child speaking clearly and with feeling. In many drama clubs children learn poetry before they embark on prose text because rhyming patterns make it easier for them to remember words. Kids can also feel more comfortable with a poem because it has an obvious beginning, middle and an end. To a small child, a play can seem to go on for ever.

The secret is to find a poem your child wants to read. It could be a verse about witches or wizards, grandad being locked in the toilet or a different take on an old nursery rhyme, such as Roald Dahl's 'Little Red Riding Hood and the Wolf'. A favourite book in our neck of the woods is 'The Spot on My Bum – Horrible Poems for Horrible Children' written by the hugely talented social-worker turned poet, Gez Walsh. Tongue twisters and limericks are great fun to practise as a family. They can give your child the confidence to make up his own rhymes and recite them aloud. Thinking up a limerick about a friend or brother can be hilarious. We had a great time devising one for each other. There are some rules though. Lines one, two and five must rhyme, as must lines three and four. Oh yes, and the best limericks always have a killer punch line. This is one of our efforts:

There was a young girl called Lucy
Whose gossip was always quite juicy
Her tales seemed so tall
But she loved telling us all
About the vicar and his latest floozie

Reading poetry out loud can be scary for children so check out IDEA 42, *Performing under pressure*, for tips on being brave.

Try another idea…

OK, it won't win any poetry awards but you can see what we're getting at. Your child could even write a poem about a big local event and send it to the newspaper's letters page. She'll get an enormous boost from seeing her work in print. Just make sure you encourage her to keep trying if her efforts are not published straightaway. Poetry is a great time-waster if you're stuck in a traffic jam. If your child likes to devise his own verse, it can be an innovative way to write or talk about a subject at school.

In June 2007, poet Michael Rosen was named Britain's Children's Laureate, replacing author Jacqueline Wilson. At the age of 12 he started writing satirical poems about people he knew.

'I've often seen and heard children writing and performing their poetry and almost every single time their pride and pleasure in doing so has been priceless,' Michael told us. 'We owe it to children to find as many occasions as possible where we can give them this kind of concentration and this kind of lift.'

'Children love poetry for the same reason they love to text each other – they can say a lot in a few words. Let's face it, two lines can be a poem and if performed properly becomes a play which captures all the fun and thrills of theatre.'
GEZ WALSH, children's poet

Defining idea…

Now there's a man who knows what he's talking about.

How did
it go?

**Q   My nine-year-old daughter thinks poetry is boring; how can
I persuade her it can be as fun as reading comics or her story
books?**

A   *There are some wonderful children's poets around so join the library and
take out a selection of books suitable for her age. One must-have is Susie
Gibbs' Poems for 9-Year-Olds. The librarian will be able to offer advice and
you will not be wasting money on poems your daughter does not enjoy.
If you read some verse to her she will soon realise how much fun poems
can be and will want to read more. There is also the Poetry Book Society in
London, which runs a children's poetry book club, selecting the best new
and backlist children's poetry for 7–11-year-olds.*

**Q   My son is not a great reader for his age, so can he still benefit
from poetry?**

A   *Many of the best children's poets have had their work recorded on to audio
books. The poems are usually read by actors who bring them to life to
entertain your child. If he listens to these in the car or at bedtime he will
hopefully be encouraged to start writing and reciting his own poems. He
could even record them onto a tape recorder and try to copy the actors he
has heard to give his speech a boost.*

14

Drama queens (and kings)

By learning acting techniques children soon ooze confidence, express themselves more clearly and have fun with other kids. It's why drama classes are booming.

The great thing about learning to act is you spend a lot of time playing games, which to parents might seem more at home within the repertoire of a children's entertainer.

The techniques employed by drama teachers up and down the land are supposed to be fun but don't be fooled. They are cleverly structured to gently encourage individual children to step into the spotlight in their own way. The best classes will develop your child's concentration, coordination and communication skills as well as his confidence, whether or not he dreams of becoming the next Daniel Radcliffe, star of the Harry Potter movies. When we were at school and saw 'drama' on the timetable it always seemed much more appealing than double chemistry. And, let's be honest, it was usually a much more enjoyable way to spend a couple of hours.

Here's an idea for you... **When your child has a friend over or is arguing with her brothers and sisters because they're bored, give them all the title of a story they know, such as *Baa Baa Black Sheep* or *Cinderella*. Ask them to think of an interesting way to perform the story. They could try it as a soap opera or even a rap song. This exercise gets kids started in drama because they are familiar with the story.**

OK, so chemists earn a lot more than most actors and probably drive nicer cars but, hey, money isn't everything.

Drama is an incredibly popular after-school and weekend activity these days, with classes for children and adults popping up in most towns and cities. The advantage kids have over their parents is that their imagination is more vivid and they're usually less inhibited. Many of us older folk have become so engrossed in work and being responsible for such boring things as paying the mortgage that we've forgotten how to play. When was the last time you pretended to be a wizard (without having a drink first)? Even shy kids play with toys and use their imagination, which is why joining a drama class can bring enormous benefits. Take one of the classic drama games, Hot Seating, which is used by professional actors to get under the skin of a new character. They will sit in a chair having questions thrown at them by the cast, such as: 'Who is your character's best friend?' or 'Why does your character want to be King?' In a local drama class a child will be asked softer, less challenging questions such as 'What would you do if you won the lottery?' This is a question every kid in the class wants to answer.

Adult actors continue to play drama games throughout their training and when they're rehearsing for shows they need to tap into the 'child' inside them. They are encouraged by directors to be childlike but not childish. To put it bluntly, if an adult actor could not play and use his imagination how would characters like Spider-Man be brought to life? A musical like *Cats* would be nothing more than a bunch of adults wondering around a stage in tight leotards and stick-on ears.

Kids adapt to drama quickly because they have strong imaginations. There is more about this in IDEA 39, *It's just my imagination.*

Try another idea...

Drama teachers will play games to show children that anyone can act, even if they have no desire to take it up professionally. The kids begin with physical exercises and work as a team to produce a play. Your child's voice and speech will also improve over time and this will help him at school and in social situations.

One of our favourite exercises you can try too is to pass your child a screwed up piece of newspaper covered in sticky tape. He must imagine it is a frightened kitten. How would he hold it and look at it? Does he talk to it? Children adapt to this kind of thinking very easily. The screwed up ball can become anything at any time. Watch his thoughts and actions change as you tell him he's now holding a spider or a smelly sock. Most drama classes advertise online or in local newspapers so it should be easy to find one near you. Your child will love it and you'll start to see his confidence improve after just a few weeks.

'Acting is the least mysterious of all crafts. Whenever we want something from somebody or when we want to hide something or pretend, we're acting. Most people do it all day long.'
MARLON BRANDO, actor

Defining idea...

How did it go?

Q **My child already attends a drama class, but when I watch from outside the door they just seem to be running around like hooligans. Are they really learning anything?**

A *Don't be too quick to write off this drama school. A good drama class should be loud! There is always lots of running about because it's often easier to start children off with the physical side of acting before attempting the mental. Many respected theatre practitioners begin training professional actors this way. The important thing is does your child come out with a smile on her face and are you seeing, even small, improvements in her confidence and social skills?*

Q **This is all very well but parents are not allowed in the class. How do I know if the teachers are any good?**

A *You should always research your child's class before enrolling her. Ask what drama qualifications the teacher has and find out where they trained. Don't be fooled into thinking you have to join a large franchise of children's drama schools to get quality teaching. There are many excellent classes running from church halls led solely by qualified professional actors. Oh, and by the way, not being allowed to watch is not unusual. This would be introducing an audience which could quickly shatter your child's confidence. Just be patient and watch for the gradual improvements in how she behaves. There will usually be a show for parents each term.*

15

Improvisation means imagination

Improvisation brings a child's dreams to life. Her mind is stimulated as she learns to think quickly and she finds it easier to interact with others.

Otherwise known as 'making it up', being able to improvise can get us out of many a tight spot in life.

During one theatre production an actor failed to appear on stage for a joint scene. His horrified fellow performer was left to ad-lib some extra lines to fill the gap and save the entire cast's blushes. Apparently the audience was none the wiser, which possibly says more about the people watching!

Improvisation is a clever little acting technique. It's basically drama without a script. As well as aiding professional actors to cope with the unexpected it helps them understand their character and how he or she relates to others in a performance. Of course, if your child can learn to improvise he will get much more out of life than

Here's an idea for you…

An ideal improvisation game for shy children is Freeze/Tag involving three kids. Give two of them a brief story outline. They could be burglars stealing a painting from a museum. After a few minutes of improvising they will run out of ideas and this is when you shout 'freeze'. They stop in the position they're in and the third child tags one of the others and takes her place and continues the scene. More reserved children enjoy this game because they can take part without the fear of making mistakes.

simply being extremely good at Let's Pretend games. As adults we tend to censor what we say, whereas children improvise naturally from the moment they start playing. When your son and his friends are pretending to be astronauts, wizards or pirates and devising a game as they go along, they're improvising.

By encouraging your child to improvise he'll become more confident in social situations and find it easier to make friends. He'll be one of the instigators of ideas for games in the playground and during physical and creative lessons in the classroom.

Like a mountain climber attached to a harness, a child who knows she can improvise in any situation will have the confidence to try new things. Her life skills and thought processes, as well as how she speaks and moves, will improve. She will also learn about the importance of working as part of a team to complete a story or game.

Making it up is one of the first skills professional actors try to master when they begin the hard slog of drama training. The best improvisations occur when the players don't think too hard about what they will say and react immediately and naturally to whatever situation is being created.

There is, however, a definite protocol in the theatre when it comes to improvisation and it should be encouraged at home. Actors are told to avoid what is called 'blocking' which means saying something negative to make it harder for your partner to respond and keep a story moving forward. For instance, if two actors are playing gardeners in a scene and one says: 'I like the look of your roses', it would be bad form if the other actor replied: 'They're not roses, they're sunflowers'. This might get a cheap laugh from the audience but it would leave the first actor feeling rather silly. A good improviser would have responded with something like: 'Thanks, but don't think I'm giving away my gardening secrets.'

Children will often 'block' their friends and work against them which is why improvisation must be practised. We've all been in the situation where our child and his friend start to argue because one of them is apparently not playing properly. Indeed, a game of soldiers between two boys will be over extremely quickly if they both shoot each other. It's a good idea to introduce props to add some realism. A child with a paper fan will find it easier to play a posh lady, whilst having a broom makes the role of a servant much more believable.

One of the main reasons improvisation is such a great confidence booster for children is because, like so many acting techniques, it's something they can never get wrong. And that's not something we just made up.

Children who can improvise find it easier to overcome their nerves when they must visit unfamiliar places. Have a read through IDEA 18, *Location, location, location* for more about this.

Try another idea...

'Being able to improvise hones and quickens your reactions and forces you to make bold choices. It's a skill which can be used to break the ice in difficult situations, increase energy and build trust between children.'

LEILA BIRCH, actress

Defining idea...

How did it go?

Q   My son enjoys playing Let's Pretend on his own and is full of imaginative ideas. However, when he has a friend to play he won't allow them to initiate any games. How can I make him accept other children's ideas?

A   Many actors have the same problem early on in their training. It's the old adage of 'Too many cooks spoil the broth'. It can be disappointing if one person comes up with a great idea only to find that the others in the group don't want to go along with it. To avoid this you can give the children a rough outline of a story before their improvising starts. Allow one child to make up the first part of the story and decide beforehand what will happen and then his friend can decide how things will move on from there and how the story will end.

Q   What about in the playground, when there is nobody to set the boundaries? Will he end up playing on his own?

A   When you're practising making up stories make sure you have an equal amount of input so he gets used to accepting other people's ideas. Try suggesting things that are very different from his normal choice of games. He'll learn that other children and adults can come up with fun ideas too. Actors are well aware that working in a team of creative minds takes practice and patience to get right.

16

Building your own character

Actors spend hours researching characters the audience will believe in. Letting your child act out different roles will help her accept who she is and understand that everyone is different.

Next time you're having trouble sleeping, don't count sheep. Compile a list of the world's greatest actors instead.

Our personal roll of honour would certainly include Sir John Gielgud. How about Sir John Mills, Marlon Brando, Alec Baldwin, Dame Judi Dench or even Tom Hanks? My goodness, we can feel our eyelids growing heavier as we write. A game for later we think. What all these actors have in common is an amazing ability to portray characters whose personalities are so different to their own. The more far-fetched the part, the more challenging and interesting it usually is for everyone watching. Who can forget Gielgud's Academy Award-winning supporting role as a mocking butler in the 1981 comedy *Arthur*?

Actors are taught to people-watch. To be observant and effectively spy on all of us in cafes or on the bus and make mental notes of particular character traits they might

Here's an idea for you...

Ask your child to imagine she's someone completely different, maybe a cartoon superhero or a witch making spells. She must speak and sit as her character. If she's a witch, get her to pose with a hunched back and spindly fingers. She must then answer questions such as, What is your name? Where do you live? and What music do you like? The longer she does this the more confident she will become as her character. This exercise makes her aware of different traits and habits that she may or may not like to adopt herself.

be able to use one day. Are you that bloke who bites his nails incessantly on the train every morning or that annoying lady who speaks particularly loudly on her mobile phone? Actors are everywhere and watching you, so beware. Personality exercises with your child can be really rewarding. Most kids are naturally sharp-eyed and will already have encountered many different 'characters' in their lives, from policemen and doctors to their own teacher and family members. There are also fictional people in books and on television whose idiosyncrasies stick in the mind.

Getting your child to take on the role of a different character for a day or even a few minutes can do wonders for her self-confidence. It's like putting on a mask and takes the pressure off being herself for a while so she can behave differently. This can be a useful way to approach situations or undertake tasks she might otherwise be nervous about. Using characters is also a good way to remove bad habits. Maybe she slouches when eating. You can ask her to sit at the table like the Queen. How would the Queen eat and what would she say to her servants (you) bringing her meal? A good way of introducing the acting technique of character building is to discuss with her some archetypal characters she knows, such as the friendly postman, her school head teacher or a famous singer. Can she stand like a frozen statue of that person? Where would they put their hands and what facial expressions would they pull? You could turn this into a game of 'Guess who?' and take it in turns to pose.

One of the hardest, but most fun, characterisations for any actor is to play a person with fundamentally different beliefs and ethics to their own. Maybe they have been chosen for the role of a thief or murderer – or even a traffic warden. The only way they can make their character convincing is to empathise with them in some way and get into their shoes mentally, however tight the fit. The actor must discover something he and the character have in common and build from there. After all, every one of us has a good and a bad side to our personality.

Copying this approach with your child will help him identify with people he personally might not like or understand but who he needs the confidence to deal with. Studying different people and their distinct characteristics will make him aware there are many types of humans in the world. It's important he understands how it feels to be someone else, with different worries, concerns and attitudes to life so he's confident around them.

Now back to that list. Robert De Niro, Clint Eastwood, Ian McKellen ... yawn.

A great way to get children interested in developing characters is to put on a show for family and friends. IDEA 26, *For one day only in the living room*, explains how kids can get a real buzz out of doing just that.

Try another idea...

'You can tell a lot about a fellow's character by the way he eats jelly beans and whether he picks one colour or just grabs a handful.'
RONALD REAGAN, former US president

Defining idea...

How did
it go?

Q   My son loves playing different characters but he has started to impersonate his teachers, which I am not so happy about. What should I do?

A   *Let's start with the positives. It's good your son is taking an interest in the way different people talk and move, but you need to rein him in on this one before he starts to cause offence and gets himself into trouble at school. The next time you're discussing characters, suggest fictional people from his favourite films or TV shows instead. Everybody enjoys watching impersonations of well-known characters and nobody will be offended!*

Q   I think he'll like that because his impersonations are usually very good. The problem is he seems to prefer putting on voices most of the time rather than being himself. Should I be worried about this?

A   *What's important is that your son is communicating with you and he may just find it easier to deal with different situations by pretending to be somebody else. If you tell him to stop he may not communicate with you at all. Many shy children like to hide behind different voices and characters when talking. This is their way of getting their points across. It's nothing to worry about.*

17

Don't argue with the director

What the director says goes in the theatre. Children can learn a lot from directing their own lives, using their initiative and taking responsibility for their own decisions.

To the untrained eye all you need to be a great director is a beard, a baseball cap and one of those fold-out chairs with your name on the back. Oh, and a megaphone.

Every stage show, film, television series and commercial has a director who must not only look the part (OK, they don't all have beards) and take responsibility for every important decision. He'll choose the actors, yell at them if they don't deliver their lines properly and decide what costumes they'll wear and what set they'll perform in front of. The director will also make cuts to the script, leaving an actor's fragile ego in pieces on the floor if his lines suddenly vanish. Many children thrive

Here's an idea for you...

Next time you and the family are fed up in the car, ask the children to imagine they are filming a documentary about boring long journeys. Allocate the quietest person the job of director. He or she can decide who will be the presenter, the bored traveller who is interviewed and even the cameraman who shouts 'action' on command. The director will decide where the programme is set, who speaks first and when to say 'cut'.

from being given the chance to 'direct' their own lives and to make executive decisions about the things that affect them.

Here's what we mean. Why not let your child take on the role of director around the house for a day? She could choose where everyone sits around the table at mealtimes, what the family eats and even what time she goes to bed. This may sound like you're condoning anarchy in the home, but it will actually give her the confidence to make decisions in her life and, more importantly, realise there are consequences. She will realise that going to bed at 11 p.m. when you are only nine years old is not so much fun if you are too tired to enjoy playing with your friends the next day. Children who learn a sense of responsibility tend to be much more self-sufficient as they grow older. If they're allowed to be in charge from time to time their self-esteem is boosted because they feel they're contributing to the household. Be prepared for your child, like a theatre director, to take her new responsibilities extremely seriously.

We remember a play where the director dragged in some live ponies to make a scene featuring some poor and dishevelled villagers more realistic. The final love scene took place in front of a carriage and right on cue the ponies decided to empty their bowels on stage. The children and the audience thought this was hilarious while the director buried his head in his hands over a spectacle he felt had ruined his show. And let's just say directors really know how to sulk. You can even allow your child to take on a theatrical director's role with her friends as the actors. She could create a short scene based at the seaside. Once the kids have performed it once, your child, as the director, can suggest changes to make the action more entertaining. She could ask her friends to repeat the action as if she has just pressed the fast-forward button or to perform it in slow motion. How about turning a speech scene into a musical?

Children feel good about themselves when they can confront personal issues on their own and take control. IDEA 37, *The solo performance*, explains how this works.

Try another idea...

This is a great exercise for children who usually prefer to remain in the background. By giving them the title of 'director' they can have their say and enjoy being the decision maker for once. This exercise also benefits the children who are the actors because it encourages them to listen and to try somebody else's ideas without being able to complain or argue. In the theatre the whole company of players must trust and respect the director, and as a parent you must avoid criticising your child while she is in charge. Like a stage director she will not deliberately make wrong decisions and will do what she believes is right to help everyone. She must feel she is in complete control and that her authority will not be questioned. She will certainly realise that to earn the respect of others a director must be fair, listen to everyone's point of view, be organised and most of all not be (too) bossy.

'Being responsible sometimes means pissing people off.'
GENERAL COLIN POWELL

Defining idea...

How did it go?

Q **My child finds it very difficult to make decisions and tends to reply to everything with the phrase 'I don't mind'. This makes my life easier but how can I get him to be more confident in explaining what he wants to do?**

A *Some children say 'I don't mind' because they are not used to being given the responsibility to make a decision. You can start by allowing your son to decide what game to play when he is bored and going along with his choice. In drama classes if a child has behaved really well they are allowed to decide what game to play to finish the session. The children are happier with this than being given a sticker for doing something the adults suggested.*

Q **Why does my son still struggle to make the association between the role of director and making his own decisions?**

A *The next time your child plays the role of director for the day, give him an imaginary hat to wear that only you two can see. Explain that the hat will give them the power to make decisions and be in charge. You can ask him to put on his imaginary hat every time he's struggling to make up his mind. To some children a real hat from your props box (see IDEA 4, Prop till you drop) will work well too – this should help your child feel more 'in character' to make up his mind confidently.*

18

Location, location, location

While actors get excited about filming somewhere exotic and adapt to their environment, children can sometimes be nervous about new places. Kids need to feel at ease when they're away from home.

Some actors spend years touring the country living out of a suitcase while others long for a three-month stint on a Caribbean cruise or a week shooting a television commercial in Barcelona.

One of the perks of being an actor is spending time on location and seeing the world. In fact, you might as well pack up and try a different career altogether if you're not prepared to travel at the drop of a hat. Wherever they are in the world, actors will make use of their surroundings. If your child can adapt quickly to her environment she'll feel more confident about visiting different places. This can certainly make your lives easier when touring a potential new school or if she's preparing for an overnight visit to relatives or friends. Children are far more likely

Here's an idea for you...

Bored kids and the rain are a lethal combination. Next time the heavens open and you are stuck in a caravan or tent, try staging a family talent show. You can select a judge, a presenter and everyone else can be various contestants who believe they have a gift. This exercise is great fun and encourages quieter children to participate in the exercise because it is meant to be silly and there is no pressure to be good. Don't forget to do it again and swap roles.

than their parents to be nervous about new locations because they're away from the things that make them feel secure, such as their friends, pets and even their bedroom. If your child is anxious about leaving home for even a few hours, turn the trip into an adventure before she goes.

Most actors will research a new location prior to beginning a tour so they know what to expect when they arrive. They want some idea of how they're going to spend their days before each evening's performance once the rehearsals have finished. They need to know where the pubs are, especially if their temporary landlady is a batty theatre nut obsessed with their show and won't leave them alone.

It can be great fun to investigate the ins and outs of a destination with your child and discover places he might want to visit. He won't be so apprehensive if he can look forward to a trip to a theme park or maybe a museum. If he's going to stay with relatives you could even ask them to produce an Entertainments Guide for him to read before he goes. You can also provide him with a tape recorder so he can keep a spoken diary of his stay. He'll really look forward to playing this to you when he returns.

When Lucy was a child she had a role in a BBC children's series which was filmed in Dorset, a long way from her home in Kent. She was only 11 and she and five other lucky children stayed in a hotel by the sea, watched over by a doddery old chaperone. The kids bonded by playing tricks on this poor woman. Ahem … not to be recommended, but helping your child to bond with other kids who might also be nervous can make him feel less homesick. If you're going away as a family it can be difficult for everyone if one child is less confident than his brother or sister about making friends. You can suggest a few questions and ideas to get your child talking to new children, such as 'Where do you live?' or 'What's your school like?' You can even give him a fun project to do on the beach, which will encourage other children to come and help him. He could create his own puppet show behind a mound of sand. The other kids will love this and want to be involved too.

Wherever you're off to, send us a postcard and let us know how you get on.

Try another idea…

A child's self-esteem can rise if she learns not to take things too seriously and shares her different experiences. You might find IDEA 32, *Knowing when to laugh or cry*, particularly useful here.

Defining idea…

'*Travel has a way of stretching the mind. The stretch comes not from travel's immediate rewards, the inevitable myriad new sights, smells and sounds, but with experiencing firsthand how others do differently what we believed to be the right and only way.*'
RALPH CRAWSHAW, US physician

How did it go?

Q   My child is quite confident and resourceful when entertaining himself at home, but whenever we go on holiday he becomes very clingy. Any ideas?

A   At many holiday resorts there are numerous activities for children so you need to find out if there's one he'll like. Increasingly, drama is being included as an activity alongside sport and arts and crafts. Maybe he will respond to that? The key is to find a resort where there will be plenty for him to do. You know his hobbies, but don't forget to show him the brochure and see if he would be keen to try something different. He might surprise you.

Q   My other child settles into new places fine during the day when we're on holiday but he won't take part in any of the children's activities in the evening. This means he is pinned to our side. Any suggestions on how to make him more confident so he'll attend events like the kids' disco?

A   You have to remember that not everyone wants to be in the limelight. There are other things he could be doing. Why not give him a disposable camera and get him to be the photographer for the evening, catching the most funky moves or capturing some of the other activities going on? This will allow him to interact with the other children as well as giving him something to do.

19

Why saying 'yes' is much more fun

Actors learn to use positive language during auditions and improvisations to keep conversations buzzing. Finding ways to boost your child's vocabulary will help him express himself more confidently.

The way you communicate and how you answer and ask questions is crucial in the cut-throat world of acting and life generally.

The first stage of many auditions is a chat with the casting director. Answer his question, 'What have you been doing lately?' with a short 'Not much,' and you'll be back at your waitressing job before the lunchtime rush has finished. A more detailed and interesting response will give the director an insight into your personality and background and *might* convince him you are right for the part.

Children who worry about what they'll say if someone poses them a question can suffer many a sweaty palm moment. Although it is impossible to pre-empt what

Here's an idea for you... **A game that children love and which encourages them to gently express their individual opinion is 'If you were a ...' and it can be played anywhere. Ask your child a series of questions such as 'If you were a colour what colour would you be?' or 'If you were an animal what would you be?' Once she's got the idea, add a supplementary question of 'Why?', which teaches her to elaborate on her answers.**

anyone will ask your child, getting him to practise responding to different questions will do wonders for his self-confidence. One easy way to encourage him to talk in more than one-word answers and keep his audience – which might be you, a teacher or a club leader – interested is to ask him to discuss his favourite book or toy. He should have no trouble chatting for 30 seconds about why he likes it, when he got it and how horrified he would be if it went missing. When he's finished, ask him some more questions but this time make a game of it by telling him he is not allowed to say just 'yes' or 'no'. In fact, tell him he must answer with a complete sentence. For instance, if you ask him 'Did you enjoy the book?' he could answer 'Yes, and I would definitely recommend it to my friend, Dominic.' This is a technique actors use during warm ups because it encourages others to follow up a response to a question with an explanation. Basically it gets people talking.

If you have a number of children playing together wait until they are sitting around the table for tea and, before the food fight starts, ask each of them a simple question such as 'Do you like school?' Again, tell them they are banned from saying simply 'yes' or 'no'. Some children will struggle with this at first because it can be less daunting to them if they are allowed to give a mono-syllable answer. Some children are too nervous to speak at all and would prefer to just nod or shake their head. What you will find is that because you have created a game, the children will rise to the challenge. The experience of drama teachers up and down the country is that with regular practise of answering easy questions, children discover it is not as scary as they thought to actually express an opinion. In fact, they find the whole exercise quite rewarding.

Talking about yourself and your life comes easier if you can express yourself well. This is explored in IDEA 5, How Now Brown Cow.

Try another idea…

For many parents, getting their children to spill the beans on what they did at school all day can be like pulling teeth and they're lucky to get anything more than a 'not much' response. If you are firing questions at your child without much reaction, again, try making it fun. Tell him that in this game 'yes' means 'no' and 'no' means 'yes'. If you ask if he had a good day at school he must answer the opposite to how he really feels. You can find your child naturally and quite unexpectedly elaborates on some answers because the questions are more game-like rather than sounding like a detective interrogating a suspect. It is a reality of modern life that youngsters who have the confidence to express an opinion and join in discussions earn the respect of others and benefit accordingly both socially and academically.

Actors are always being encouraged to think differently and to voice their views without fear of being interrupted or put down. It is important children are too.

'They say the world has become too complex for simple answers. They are wrong.'

RONALD REAGAN

Defining idea…

How did it go?

Q   **My child is reluctant to talk and when he does he is constantly saying 'um' and 'er'. Is this just a sign of a small vocabulary?**

A   *This is extremely common in children and some adults so be careful not to draw attention to this habit or he will become even more nervous about speaking. You can overcome it. Ask one member of the family to talk about a topic they know a lot about. It could be their hobby or something they are learning at school. Mums and dads can take part in this too. The rules of the game are that the person speaking is not allowed to say 'um' or 'err'. If they do it is someone else's turn. This game will highlight to your child how often they hesitate and it should gradually help to eradicate the habit.*

Q   **Won't this make my child feel more insecure about the way he communicates?**

A   *As with all drama games the emphasis must be on fun so your child should be unaware that the game is directed at him. You could introduce a host in the style of a TV show who is allowed to say 'Beep' every time someone says 'Um'. This makes the game even more enjoyable and takes the pressure off exactly what you are trying to achieve.*

20

Let's get physical

Kids are confident about their bodies if they have good coordination skills and are aware of their personal space. You can even tell a person's mood by the way they move.

It is one of those 'yuck' moments when a complete stranger gets so close on the bus that you can smell his body and feel his breath upon your face.

We all love our personal space. Don't ask us for a scientific definition of what exactly this is but it's basically an invisible area around each one of us, which, if invaded, makes us nervous or embarrassed. If actors are not spatially aware on stage a show can become extremely messy. A child gains in confidence as his individual spatial awareness improves. Younger kids learn to judge distances and develop a sense of direction if they understand how the things around them relate to where they are standing. The stains on the carpets and broken ornaments in our house are testament to how this can take a while to get right.

In physical theatre the story is told mainly through bodily movements rather than the text. The performers must be conscious of how their bodies move and have excellent coordination skills. The best physical actors bring characters to life simply by emulating how a person would walk or gesture. Children will feel more confident if they can improve their posture. A child who slouches with his arms crossed and rarely moves around in the playground can appear unapproachable to other kids.

There are numerous physical exercises actors employ to make them more aware of their bodies and the space around them. These can work wonders with children too. Simple things like rolling the shoulders and bending the neck from side to side (don't lean the neck backwards as this can damage the coccyx) can loosen up the body. Really tensing the arms and relaxing them after a couple of seconds and repeating this with different parts of the body such as legs and buttocks (clench and release – stop laughing at the back) also works. You can use more visual ideas with younger children. Tell them to walk tall and straight as a soldier or like a spaceman on the moon.

Actors find a comfortable standing position by slumping forwards so their arms are almost touching the floor. They then slowly come up to a standing position by straightening the spine. Your child could be a closed flower that gradually comes to life. Quick tip here: he will be more inclined to move if music is played.

Here's an idea for you... **Make some basic masks, just cardboard with the eyes and mouth cut out. Attach these to your child and her friends with string. The children cannot speak or use facial expressions to communicate. They can only use their physical bodies. Tell them they've arrived on a new planet for the first time. How do they feel and move around? Do they explore or are they too scared? This will develop their awareness of how they move. Masks also give shy children the confidence to perform because they have a disguise to hide behind.**

Performers also shake out their arms and feet frantically to remove any tension and relax their muscles. This is a great one if you need your child to stand still for something important. Remember the time you went to church and he did nothing but fiddle? Before you go next time get him to wiggle his body and run about like a mad thing to get any urge to fidget out of his system. This technique can also be used to remove any nervous energy if your child is waiting to read or perform in public.

There are plenty of physical drama games your child will love. How about Port/Starboard where the 'captain' is blindfolded and placed behind his 'helmsman'. The Captain must give directions such as 'port' (turn left) and 'starboard' (turn right). It's great fun for the kids to see where they end up in the room.

Then there's the Beans Game. Tell your children to be jelly beans and wobble, runner beans and run or coffee beans where they must drink coffee like parents in a café.

Actors are taught how to make fights look realistic. These brawls are carefully choreographed so no-one gets hurt. You can devise one at home as an effective way to teach kids self-control. They will soon understand there are boundaries that shouldn't be crossed in physical games.

Try another idea...

Physical movements can really help shy children to communicate which is why mime is such a winner. IDEA 25, *Mime the gap*, is well worth a read.

Defining idea...

'*Every child has a body and a voice. Music and speech involve the whole child. Music should be a central part of all childhood experiences, creating self-confidence before children discover self-consciousness.*'

DIDI BRIGGS,
Pre-School Music Association

How did it go?

Q **My daughter attends an after-school activity club but came home last week and told me another child had made bodily contact with her during a physical exercise. Surely this should be discouraged?**

A *On the contrary. Kids need be comfortable with their bodies so they don't freak out if they touch another child. Actors often have to play someone's wife or daughter and it would not be very real if the person stiffened when they were given a hug. Ask your child and a friend to stand close to each other. Get them to press their palms together and to put pressure on each other through the hands and fingers. Then ask them to release the tension slightly until they're only just touching with their fingers. This teaches children different levels of touch and requires plenty of concentration.*

Q **These are young children. How can I be sure things won't get out of hand and my daughter won't get hurt by playing physical games?**

A *Any good teacher or club leader will not embark on physical exercises unless the kids are properly supervised and he is sure the children know the boundaries. There should not be any aggressive behaviour which would make your daughter feel uncomfortable. We are talking about hugging not fighting.*

21

You're not helping, Mum

**'Don't put your daughter on the stage Mrs Worthington',
wrote Noel Coward. Indeed, parents who try to fulfil
their dreams through their children can knock their
confidence.**

There was a great film at the end of
the eighties called *Beaches* where the
child character Cecilia Carol Bloom suffers from
the embarrassing antics of her overbearing stage
mother.

In the world of performing arts a stage mother is a child actor's mum who is convinced her kid has immense talent. She will drive her son or daughter to numerous auditions but – and this is the crucial bit – put an unacceptable amount of pressure on them to succeed. A rise in the number of television talent shows and the possible riches available to top sportsmen and women can mean children are sometimes forced to try things they secretly hate. It can create the ridiculous scenario where

Here's an idea for you... **Actors are always encouraged to talk about childhood experiences to help them form different characters. Next time you are chatting with adult friends, start a conversation about your own parents and your friends' parents. What positive and negative traits did they have that have rubbed off on you? Do you remember your parents making you do something you hated when you were young?**

they attend a club just to please their mum or dad. Yet if they are not enjoying themselves and are, frankly, not very good at the activity their confidence can nosedive.

The reality in the theatre and in sport is that few children succeed thanks to pushy parents. This is largely because it is so damn hard to get work as an actor and to reach the top in a particular sport that a person will fail without single-minded determination and a high level of confidence in their own ability.

It is not only over-ambitious parents who can knock children's confidence. A mother who is blatantly nerv-ous about her child visiting somewhere or taking part in a new activity can pass on her jitters to her offspring. Kids need to feel their parents are relaxed about things in life, even if in reality their mother's stomach is turning cartwheels. If you are worried about something, don't display your own anxiety. Instead try to 'act' confident and rehearse in your mind what you will say when, for example, you're driving your son to his new school. Tell him how exciting it will be, the great things he will do and the new friends he's going to meet.

One of the best ways to calm your nerves and avoid showing your child how worried you are is to breathe properly. Take a peek at IDEA 2, *The ins and outs of breathing.*

Try another idea…

Here's a classic example. From our experience of drama clubs, some parents will bring their child along and in front of her tell the teacher how nervous she is and then start cuddling and holding her whilst repeatedly asking her if she is OK. If she had been left at the door the teacher would have made sure she was included from the start and she'd probably be fine.

Many actors will recite a mantra before going on stage and you can devise your own one. How about 'She will be fine … she will be fine …' and repeat it a few times once you have dropped off your child at the school gates or club house. If you are really worried you can always sit outside in the car for a few

'Children begin by loving their parents; as they grow older they judge them; sometimes they forgive them.'

OSCAR WILDE

Defining idea…

minutes just in case there really is a problem. Some parents get annoyed when they're told they can't sit in and watch their child's drama or gym class. Yet it is hard enough for shy children to perform in front of others without introducing an audience, especially if their parents are in the front row.

Similarly, if your child enjoys being part of a group but is still learning a routine or skill, don't insist they sing, dance or try juggling for Auntie Edith and Uncle Bryan when they visit for Sunday lunch. After all, you wouldn't ask him to recite his seven times table during a family party would you? Or maybe you would. Your child's self-belief can also be shattered if his friend has been put up a grade and you feel some sort of parental peer pressure to insist your kid moves up too. The danger here is that your child will lose his confidence to do an activity which he previously enjoyed because he suddenly finds it too difficult.

Q   **When my daughter fell over at ballet and grazed her knee I took**
     her home and treated her like a princess for the rest of the day.
     We've talked about what happened and the dangers of dancing
     but I worry she has been put off. Should I encourage her to try
     something different?

How did it go?

A   *I am sure professional dancers, even the great Darcey Bussell, fall over from*
     time to time. They just get back up and carry on. It is parental instinct to
     make a fuss of a child following an accident. However, her confidence will
     not return if she thinks ballet dancing is dangerous. If she really enjoys
     ballet then encourage her to return and explain how occasionally even the
     best dancers take a tumble.

Q   **So should I tell her dance teacher to treat her with care from**
     now on, especially during her first session back?

A   *Actually the more you play down this incident the better. She will be aware*
     you have sneaked into the room and had a quiet word with the teacher.
     She will probably not thank you if she is treated differently from the other
     children in the class who might then resent her in some way. Ironically she
     will become more confident about dancing once she knows she can cope
     with a fall. In fact, you might even see her progress more rapidly.

22

Great concentrations

Concentration is crucial on stage and helping your child to improve his attention span can do wonders for his self-confidence.

An actor who has played the same role for weeks can suddenly discover during an important and emotional monologue that he's forgotten to feed his cat that evening.

When this happens the performance can suddenly become unbelievable because the audience can tell the actor's mind is wandering. As harsh as it might sound, they will not care that he has a stomach-rumbling feline starving at home. Actors also need to follow closely what others are saying and doing on stage so they know precisely when to speak and move. To avoid embarrassing lapses of concentration they'll practise different techniques to remain focused. Concentration is linked to listening and communication skills, and a child who remains attentive at school tends to do well because she doesn't have to keep asking her teachers to repeat things.

We all get nervous when we find something difficult in life, especially if we haven't listened to the instructions. Before driving a huge motor home around California

Here's an idea for you...

Get your child and some of his friends to stand in a circle. Give them an imaginary radar gun and tell them they can 'zip' the person opposite them and 'zap' the people either side of them. They can send a shot back to where it came by saying 'boing'. This is a warm-up game used by actors to build concentration because everyone is involved and no-one can switch off for a second.

we had to sit through a 20-minute how-to-do-it presentation. It was all rather dull at the time and it was only when we were ready to drive off we realised we'd not been paying attention and the panic set in. Just how do you get rid of your sewage when you're 7,000m up in Yosemite National Park?

Actors play a quick-fire game called Word Tennis to boost their concentration levels before a rehearsal or performance. Try it with your child. If one of you says 'table' another must reply instantly with a related word such as 'chair'. This game requires 100% concentration because a player loses if they repeat a word or hesitate for a split second. Actors will often slice up parts of a script to help them learn different lines, and children can find it much easier to concentrate on things if they are split into threes.

If your child is nervous about a Show and Tell at school where she'll be expected to enlighten the class on the joys of owning a pet hamster, try breaking down what she will say into three parts.

Firstly she can practise introducing the hamster's name and describing her furry friend, secondly she can talk about why she likes her hamster and thirdly she can ask if anyone has any questions. Events can seem much less daunting if they are handled like this.

Actors also use the Concentration Circles technique based on the teaching of renowned drama guru, Konstantin Stanislavski. He believed people concentrate differently in different situations, which he called Circles. All a bit 'out-there' we know but, hey, it seems to work. There are three circles actors use. The first is when they are alone, circle two is if another character is there and circle three is when more people are involved. By using the circle idea you can highlight to your child how he can present himself differently. This takes a lot of concentration but should be fun. Mark three areas or circles on the floor and tell him he must talk in a whisper in circle one, speak moderately loudly in the second circle and very loudly when he's in the third. Give him a simple poem to try or get him and a friend to stand in different circles and hop between all three whilst having a conversation.

This technique works because whatever situation your child is in he can relate back to the circle idea. When speaking in class he can imagine he's in circle three or if he's being noisy somewhere he shouldn't you can ask him politely to pretend he's in circle one.

Sounds a bit complicated but it does work. You can practise different role plays at home or in the car until he really understands the idea.

Concentration is crucial when your child is in a pressurised situation so take a look at IDEA 42, *Performing under pressure*, for more tips.

Try another idea…

'If you can keep playing tennis when somebody is shooting a gun down the street that is concentration.'
SERENA WILLIAMS

Defining idea…

How did it go?

Q **In my son's school report the teacher noted how he has a short attention span of only five minutes at best. My son says he just gets bored quickly, so how can I make him realise that he will benefit if he concentrates harder?**

A *The great thing about concentration is that it can be practised and developed over time. The important thing is that any acting-related exercises you try must be fun. Try the game called 30 Second Lists. Give him just half a minute to name as many football teams or sweets as he can. You can then progress to a minute on different subjects. This is basically brain training but he will respond because he will see it as a competition and he will want to beat you!*

Q **I hear what you're saying but my son is only six. Isn't it natural for boys to find it harder than girls to concentrate at school at such a young age? Isn't this just something that will improve as he gets older?**

A *There may be something in this but, again, boys will respond more to games and techniques they can relate to. They tend to like more physical games so try a round of Simon Says (for example, 'Simon says pretend to be a monster'), which is great for holding boys' concentration and for burning off energy. Many younger boys even struggle with something as simple as standing still so you must persevere when attempting to improve their attentiveness.*

23

Keeping a lid on anger

**Actors love aggressive roles, and when your child gets
angry she needs to know how she can let off steam.**

*You will find actors almost salivating with
anticipation when they are given a scene
with a good old argument and a bit of
high drama.*

They love the chance to rant at another character because everyone has the experience of being outraged and downright furious. Remember how cross you felt when that awful woman from number 12 stole your parking space? Playing a baddie is fun, although surprisingly tiring because it takes a lot of physical effort to breathe and project your voice correctly to convey anger on stage. Hard to believe when you consider how much you hear when your neighbours are rowing.

While most adults know how to channel their frustrations, many children get nervous about expressing their anger and consequently bottle everything up. This is a mistake because they end up walking around like a ticking time bomb ready

Here's an idea for you...

One of the best ways to help your child overcome her anger is to act out a scene where she swaps roles with the person she's cross with. If she has been wrongly accused of talking in class and made her teacher angry, set up a little play where she is the teacher and you and her siblings are the naughty children. She will soon realise how hard it is for a teacher to keep control, and how mistaken identity can easily happen.

to explode at any minute. They often 'go off' in the wrong place such as the school playground and they are the ones who get into trouble. One thing that makes kids really mad is not having their say. The most confident children tend to be those who can express their anger and who say something at the time rather than letting problems stagnate.

In the theatre the director will try to dilute any tension during rehearsals by giving everyone in the cast the chance to voice their opinion without the fear of being interrupted. You can try this at home when there is something which has infuriated your child. She could be annoyed about a toy which has gone missing or cross that her brother has got something she hasn't. Let everyone in the family speak for a couple of minutes. You'll be amazed how much more confident your child will be about getting something off her chest when she's sure no one will butt in. She will keep her self-control because she knows she has a listening audience.

There is also the 30-second rant exercise which actors use to get into an angry frame of mind before they play an irate character. Tell your child she can shout and holler as much as she likes about something that's annoyed her. Again, resist the urge to interject. Is she fed up with the amount of homework she gets or the time she must go to bed? You'll probably discover she cannot actually remain seething for the full 30 seconds and she'll end up laughing. What's important is that she feels a lot better about everything because she's had the confidence to explain what has upset her.

Children get angry when they are disappointed. Have a read through IDEA 45, *Next! Why is life so unfair?*, for tips on dealing with this.

Try another idea…

If she has been given the opportunity to meet with someone, maybe a teacher, to discuss something which has distressed her, it is a good idea to write down three or four things she might otherwise forget to mention when she's sitting in the room feeling nervous. When an actor is considering how he will play an angry character he'll often scribble down reasons why that person is so annoyed.

Younger children can also use puppets to express their anger about something that's happened. Maybe they're being teased at school or haven't been invited to a party? Your child can make basic puppets out of paper or use his favourite toys. He can hide behind the sofa which acts as the perfect stage. If your child is having problems expressing his feelings at school, choose a school-related title for the show. How about something simple like 'The Teacher'? Children, like actors, will naturally use their own experiences to act out scenes. Under the guise of a puppet your child will express his feelings towards his teacher or a friend and release some of the built-up resentment and tension that might otherwise remain locked up.

'Temper is the only thing you cannot get rid of by losing it.'
JACK NICHOLSON as Dr Buddy Rydell in the 2003 movie *Anger Management*

Defining idea…

How did it go?

Q **My daughter is quite shy but she still gets very cross within herself when she is not picked for certain jobs and responsibilities in the classroom. Will this affect her confidence when it comes to volunteering in future because she feels it's not worth putting up her hand?**

A *People can wrongly assume that because a person is shy they do not want to be in the spotlight and this can mean they get overlooked. Encourage your child to approach her teacher on her own and to ask if one day she could be the milk monitor or take the register to the office. To steady her nerves you can even rehearse beforehand how this chat would go and what she should say.*

Q **Won't the teacher find such an approach irritating and get cross herself?**

A *If you don't ask in life you don't get. Actors are always advised to put their necks on the line and be confident enough to ask for the best parts. When extra lines are being handing out by the director it is often the person who shouts the loudest who gets them. It is not always easy for a child to push herself forward to get noticed but with practice and by using different techniques it will become easier. Your daughter's teacher will probably be pleased she has brought the matter to her attention, as long as she chooses the right moment to mention it.*

24

Making sense of it all

By exploring the five senses of touch, taste, smell, sight and hearing in a fun way, your child will get a better understanding of her own body and the world around her.

From touchy-feely exercises to help actors warm up, to the smell of old costumes and amazing sound and lighting effects, the theatre keeps our senses incredibly busy.

There is no doubt that a child whose senses are sharp will feel and act with confidence. She'll see and hear what's going on around her and, when it comes to taste, will be more confident to try new foods. A blessing for any parent worried their child will waste away because she is a fussy eater and lives on fish fingers and yoghurt. Certain smells will remind her of good and bad experiences in her life and jog her memory about how she has coped with different situations before.

Obviously actors are very aware of how they can and should use their senses. Such feelings are crucial to playing any role because performers must be conscious of

Here's an idea for you... **If you have a recording device, plan and perform a radio cookery programme with your child. With no visual element you must both describe tastes and smells and talk about the texture of the food. What does it look like raw and cooked? Encourage your child to use as much detail as possible. Maybe the ice cream 'melts on the tongue'. You can also produce a visual show using a camcorder.**

everything going on around them. Professional theatres will have a sound department to monitor the actors' voices when they're singing or speaking. Actors who have never met before must be comfortable with touching each other if they are playing members of the same family. When it comes to dinner table scenes where real food is involved, an actor must master the art of tasting and eating realistically whilst not being caught chewing when it's his turn to speak. In fact, such scenes are usually carefully choreographed to avoid the ugly sight of one actor inadvertently spitting the contents of his mouth all over another character. There are many drama techniques you can use to improve your child's awareness of her senses.

- *Touch*: actors warm up for a rehearsal or a performance by touching each other to build up trust. Get your child to close her eyes and ask her sister or friend to do little taps on her back like rain or draw a number. Can she guess what's happening?
- *Taste*: put five food items in a box but don't let your child see them. Now blindfold her and ask her to pick one at a time and try it. Can she guess what it is?
- *Smell*: similarly put five items that whiff a little into a box (best to do this one after the food game for obvious reasons!). Grab your teenage son's smelly socks,

an onion, a rose petal and maybe an eraser. Your child can sniff each one but not touch. Can she guess the aroma? Just wait for the giggles.

■ *Sight*: get her and a friend to stare at each other for one minute. When the time is up, one of them must leave the room. The remaining child must subtly alter something about their appearance. Maybe remove their glasses or turn up their jeans. How quickly can the other one notice what has changed? Being observant is a real skill in life.

■ *Hearing*: ask your child to close her eyes and create an atmosphere using only her voice. Maybe she is at the beach, a farm or in outer space? If playing this game with friends she could develop her thoughts into a short play. A shy child in the group could be the sound man or woman orchestrating the noises during the performance.

The five senses can fuel your child's imagination. Take a look at IDEA 39, *It's just my imagination*, for suggestions on how to do this.

Try another idea...

What's fascinating about developing your child's senses is that you often realise that her sense of smell is stronger than her sense of taste, or vice versa. You can then address any weaknesses which were, unknown to you or her, affecting her confidence. Theme parks promote themselves on being able to thrill all our senses and we love them for it. It is the same reason the senses are so important to actors and why your child should spend time honing hers.

'Nothing can cure the soul but the senses, just as nothing can cure the senses but the soul.'

OSCAR WILDE

Defining idea...

107

How did it go?

Q **I'm convinced my son's social development is being held back by his reluctance to try new foods. It is even making me nervous about letting him visit his friends' homes after school. Is there a solution?**

A *When actors attend auditions for television commercials they often have to eat things they don't like – they wouldn't get the job if they screwed up their face during an ad for prawns. Create a mealtime game where your child pretends to like something as part of a TV commercial. Use real food you would like him to eat. If he manages to eat it, make sure you reward him in the same way an actor would be rewarded by getting the part in the advert.*

Q **But my child is even nervous about just touching different foods. How do I get over this if he does not like the texture or the smell?**

A *Ah, this one's quite easy. Devise themed meal times. You could create a cowboy or medieval banquet, where people did eat with their fingers. You can act out roles as a family with your child playing the part of the servant serving the food at the king's banquet and responsible for trying everything first to ensure it isn't poisonous. Having a banquet means you can include lots of different foods. You can also decorate the room and invite some of your son's friends who do like to eat different things as a way to encourage your child to be more adventurous.*

25

Mime the gap

Every actor strives to conquer mime, a discipline ideal for helping shy children communicate. It is often the vital first step to giving a child the confidence to talk openly to others.

Mime is basically acting without words; yet copying movements or expressions is not as easy at it sounds, although shy kids can thrive when they try it.

There have been some great mime artists over the years. One of our favourites is the late Marcel Marceau whose own hero, Charlie Chaplin, along with the likes of Buster Keaton and Harold Lloyd, learned the craft of mime in the theatre before making it big in silent movies. If your child is nervous about speaking in front of others then mime can build his confidence because it's his body rather than his tongue which is doing the talking. There is a famous German theatre chap called Bertolt Brecht who actors rave about. He told performers not to even think about a character's mental mannerisms until they understand a person's physical traits. He argued that you need to mime a person's job to really get a feel for how they behave, move and subsequently speak. Getting a postman's cheery 'Good morning' spot on is easier if you practise the happy and brisk walk that most posties have. We just wish ours wouldn't whistle quite so loudly early in the morning.

When an actor is playing a non-speaking part, maybe she's sitting in the background during a bar scene, it is her miming actions which determine whether her performance is believable. She must

Here's an idea for you…

Actors use a technique called Frozen Pictures to develop the physical attributes of a character. Ask your child to look at a picture or a painting with people in it and then to think of a title for a new one. It could be called The Storm or The Teddy Bear's Picnic. Get her to think about how she would stand if she was in that picture. She and her friends could all be in the image and when you say 'action' they start to mime and bring the picture to life.

look like she is drinking wine even if her glass is actually filled up with cheap apple juice from the local supermarket. Children can be very self-conscious about their bodies and it's often their body language, such as the way they are standing or how they hunch up of their shoulders, which can expose their nerves. By practising mime with your child he will get used to relaxing his arms and legs and, over time, become less reserved. Actors will mime walking on different pretend surfaces such as hot coals, a sponge and then mud. Getting your child to do this will gradually make him less sensitive about movement and free any built-up tension in his body. When we've introduced mime as a game at a child's birthday party it has brought hilarious results. You can ask the guests to mime crossing a fast-flowing river on stepping stones or trying to eat an ice cream whilst walking across a wobbly bridge. From our experience even shy children love to take part because this is a game. You can even award prizes.

The effort needed to mime effectively can help kids forget their nerves. Have a quick read through IDEA 22, *Great concentrations*, to help your child pay attention.

Try another idea…

'I was that shy child and when I learned there was an art form not focused on speaking I knew it was for me. My goal is to make children realise how mime is part of their every day. Gesture has meaning. In fact, mime is the original human language.'
BILL BOWERS, American mime artist

Defining idea…

111

Young children also love being asked to mime their mum or dad's job and seeing if their friends can guess what it is. In a way this is just a version of the party game Charades except the child is told what subject to act out. Nervous children who attend drama groups but are reluctant speakers can be happy to mime going around the supermarket and buying the shopping.

What is really interesting is how they love to show and tell everyone else what is in their basket as their imagination replaces their nerves.

Although children enjoy mime don't expect them to be really good at it straight away. Tell your child to really think that they are doing something for real. If they are climbing a ladder where are they putting their feet?

You could say this is all about mime over matter. We'll get our coats.

Q   **My daughter is a real giggler and gets really embarrassed when we play different mime games with her friends or cousins. How can I get her to take these exercises seriously?**

How did it go?

A   *A great way to solve this problem and make her less self-conscious is to introduce music. Build up a collection of different types of music and play it very loudly as you ask her to move around to the style of the music. The thunderous sound of a marching band will make her instinctively want to stride around the room, whilst playing a soft lullaby, will help her to mime the act of a mother putting a baby to bed. The music acts as both a focus and a tool to remove any embarrassment your daughter obviously feels. Just make sure the neighbours are out before you crank up the volume.*

Q   **But surely having music blaring through the speakers will make it harder to develop the use of mime as a way to gradually improve her speech?**

A   *In the theatre and movies music is used a lot to enhance the action without it spoiling your enjoyment. Think of the music used in horror films. You could even introduce music to a mime to develop a short play. Your daughter could be a little goblin who has to cast a spell every time the music is played. The music does not have to be the main feature; just use it as a sound effect to inspire the action of mime and, ultimately, speech.*

26

For one day only in the living room

Most children love to put on a show for their friends and family, and the sense of achievement they feel from the positive feedback they get can be immense.

The stage at home may be more new carpet than New York, but there is a confidence-building role for everyone when children come together to perform.

Most professional shows are created in three mad weeks when actors and the back-stage crew work tirelessly to produce a piece of art that people will pay to see and hopefully tell their friends about. Whilst the actors rehearse for hours and costumes are made, the sound and lighting teams familiarise themselves with the script and the set, and choreographers compose dance and fight scenes. Reality in the theatre is all very well but no one wants to witness real blood gushing from an open wound because a struggle onstage has gone wrong. There is pressure on everyone in the

Here's an idea for you...

Get children to think beyond the traditional nativity play at Christmas and to put on a show based around busy elves making presents to meet Santa's deadline. Take them to a charity shop to buy costumes and props, and plan rehearsals. They could produce a printed programme listing everyone's names and jobs in the credits and make posters to promote the show. They could also print tickets to sell to the grown-ups.

theatre and although tempers will fray occasionally, strong friendships are made. Each person's job is important if the curtain is to go up on time. The same is true when a group of children decide to put on a play for a special family occasion or as a school holiday project.

Even if your child lacks the confidence to be one of the actors she can help to write the script, be the director or set designer, or take charge of make-up. She could even choreograph a short dance routine. There are many roles without which the performance would not be so successful. The team ethics involved in putting on a drama production will raise every child's self-esteem because there are always obstacles to overcome. Everyone who is involved, whatever job they've taken on, can share his or her ideas so the final result is the best it can be. What's essential is that your child takes on a role which challenges her. It would be a blatantly missed opportunity to boost her confidence if you allowed her to hide in the background playing a tree during the opening scene set in the woods.

Putting on a show can be a great way to celebrate a family occasion. See IDEA 48, *Birthdays can bring happy returns*, for party tips.

Try another idea...

Deciding when to put on a performance can be tricky. Christmas or birthdays are obvious candidates, so too are barbecues attended by friends and neighbours. A show can be put together in an afternoon or used as an alternative to hiring a children's entertainer.

The plot for any masterpiece also requires careful thought. The children could devise a script from scratch but this can lead to squabbling. You might prefer to suggest they go for an old favourite and adapt the plot. Parables from the Bible or fairytales and nursery rhymes are always a hit. Alternatively the kids

'From the start it has been the theatre's business to entertain people. It needs no other passport than fun.'
Acting guru BERTOLT BRECHT,
A Short Organum for the Theatre

Defining idea...

could put on an old-style variety show with different acts. You must be prepared to step in and help if they are losing enthusiasm or beginning to argue. If you're there to support them with different ideas they're more likely to remain keen. Very young children will love putting on a show too but they obviously have their limitations and get bored extremely quickly. Something short and sweet like an adaptation of Little Red Riding Hood should be the limit of your ambitions for the under sixes. This still allows plenty of scope for fun costume- and set-making.

Whatever show the children produce it will be an entertaining experience for the participants and the audience. Make sure you have the camcorder ready so you can replay the event over and over again. When your child is feeling nervous about something in future you can watch the DVD and remind her of what she achieved when she put on this splendid show with their friends. Watch the smile return to her face.

Q   I'm sure my child would love to invite her mates over and put on a play but the thought of having ten kids in my living room fills me with horror. Should I persuade her to produce the show at a friend's house?

How did it go?

A   *This would be the easy way out. If it's your child who's lacking in confidence it's important you keep control over what she's doing. You need to make sure your daughter has a role in the production which she is happy with and which will test her abilities and potential, even if she does not want to be the leading lady. The time of year could also make a difference. If your house is not big enough wait until the summer and let the children perform in the local park. Open air theatre is very prestigious these days. You could even bring a picnic and make a day of it.*

Q   That's all very well but what if it rains on the day of this great outdoor production and where are they supposed to rehearse?

A   *You must be prepared to take the kids to the park for a few Sundays to rehearse. This is a great way for them to let off steam and use up spare energy. In London, Regent's Park Open Air Theatre has been putting on shows since 1932, but if the weather is bad the performance is postponed and rescheduled for another day. The children will be disappointed so make sure you keep the next Saturday or Sunday free just in case the worst happens.*

27

Attention please, no upstaging here, thank you!

Performers are told not to draw the audience's attention away from another actor. Similarly, children must have the confidence to allow others their moment in the spotlight.

Imagine being transfixed by Romeo and Juliet's big balcony scene when all of a sudden an actor playing a passer-by begins staggering like Quasimodo from *The Hunchback of Notre Dame.*

It would probably be hilarious but it would kill the moment during what is arguably the most poignant love scene in theatre. It would also almost certainly be the last time our deformed bell-ringer impersonator worked for a while. It is often said that the more senior the actor in any production the more likely he is to complain

Here's an idea for you... **Put on a pretend fashion show for your child and their friends or siblings. One is the model and another, maybe the less confident child, is the host. The model cannot speak while the host describes how lovely the model looks and what she is wearing and asks for a twirl. The model is the star here but cannot speak or respond to what the host is saying. Repeat the exercise by swapping roles.**

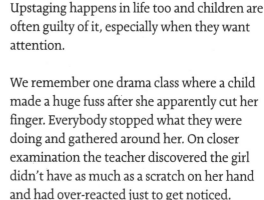

about others trying to hog the limelight during their big speech or entrance. You can call it insecurity if you like, but any form of upstaging is frowned upon in the theatre. Upstaging happens in life too and children are often guilty of it, especially when they want attention.

We remember one drama class where a child made a huge fuss after she apparently cut her finger. Everybody stopped what they were doing and gathered around her. On closer examination the teacher discovered the girl didn't have as much as a scratch on her hand and had over-reacted just to get noticed.

At school, children will upstage each other by shouting out the answer to a question which a teacher has asked someone else. This may not seem very serious but it can become an anti-social trait that encourages adults to deliberately ignore a child because he or she is perceived to have bad manners. A child who is prone to upstaging others usually lacks the self-confidence to wait until it is her turn to comment or perform a task. This could be because she has to fight to have her say at home where her brothers and sisters are much more assertive. Or she feels his parents never really listen to her or ask for her point of view.

There are many different drama techniques designed to give children the confidence to realise they don't always have to be the centre of attention. These include the type of listening games actors play which highlight how everyone involved in a production is important to its success and should be treated with respect. Try these:

- Get the family together and allow each person in turn to talk about a subject that everyone feels passionate about. The question could be 'What is the most disgusting food you've ever tasted?' The temptation for children to butt in can be enormous but the rules are strict. If someone does interrupt they miss their turn and have to wait until the next subject. They cannot even make comments such as 'so do I' or 'I agree'. There's no limit on how long someone can speak which can be unbearable for a child desperate to be in the spotlight.

When children have trust in those around them they are less likely to seek attention at their friends' expense. There is more on this in IDEA 10, *We should always trust our instincts.*

Try another idea…

'As a child, I was taught that it was bad manners to bring attention to yourself and to never, ever make a spectacle of yourself. All of which I've earned a living doing.'
AUDREY HEPBURN

Defining idea…

123

- Another exercise actors use to build confidence and trust in each other is to stand in a circle and close their eyes. As a group they must then count to ten but only one person can say each number at a time. If two people say a number simultaneously the group must go back to zero. This is much harder than it sounds.
- Find a long stick in the garden and get two children to stand at opposite ends and hold the stick with their index finger only. They have to move around and work together because if one child tries to dominate the stick will fall.

Children who seek attention tend to be insecure about their role in a group and this can lead to bad behaviour. Practising listening games will improve their social skills and subsequently their confidence as they make more friends and they are viewed positively by adults.

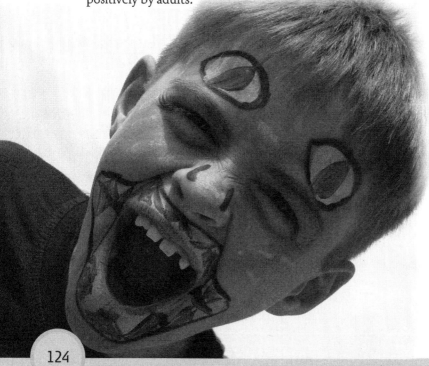

Q **Are you saying that my daughter, who can be quite loud, should take more of a back seat in group situations?**

How did it go?

A *Absolutely not. We want her to have the confidence to be an active member of the group and contribute ideas but she must be able to listen to others as well as express her own point of view. This is not about restraining her enthusiasm but about building her confidence in other people.*

Q **At the moment she is always getting noticed. Won't this different approach mean she misses out on things because the teacher fails to spot her?**

A *There is a distinct difference between shouting out and controlling the situation and learning to listen and still being a part of what's happening. Adults can ignore a child who is seeking attention and shouts out to try and hog the limelight. By being more restrained she might actually get extra opportunities to help in school. It's vital that actors listen to each other so they can respond appropriately on stage, especially if one of them makes a mistake. There's a concentration and listening exercise actors play which you could try at home. Everyone sits in a circle and listens to sounds in the room and then to sounds outside of the room. Afterwards each person describes what they heard without interruptions from the others. Did people hear different things?*

28

Tapping into your child's talents

Actors are told to play to their strengths and not audition for unsuitable roles. Your child's confidence will soar if he's encouraged to get better at the things he already excels at.

There are some roles that just suit certain actors. Think about it. Could you really see Arnold Schwarzenegger playing Heathcliff in a film adaptation of Emily Brontë's *Wuthering Heights?*

No one is disputing the Governor of California's acting ability for one minute but Arnie found a niche. He focused on playing characters that suited his bodybuilding skills and as such movies like *Total Recall* and *The Terminator* were massive hits. Of course actors fear being typecast and don't want to be crammed into a professional pigeon-hole – and what a squeeze it would be for Arnie! Yet many thespians have made a very nice living, thank-you, by concentrating on what they're good at.

Get your child to make up a television commercial about something in the house, maybe some bananas in the fruit bowl. What must she say to make people buy them? Then tell her to make an advertisement about herself. She must not say anything negative but focus on her good points. Why should people have her as a friend? Does she have a good sense of humour? This is a great exercise you can do anywhere. She could even record a pretend radio or TV advertisement for herself.

We're not suggesting for one moment that your child shouldn't try new things. On the contrary, he must be encouraged to challenge himself. What we're saying is that when it comes to feeling confident he needs to be aware of what makes him special and what things in life he can do – and let's not be modest here – better than most kids he knows. What gets him noticed in life? If he was a product on the supermarket shelf why would people buy him rather than one of his classmates?

After a year at drama school actors are usually asked what they felt about the rest of the students when they first met them. This exercise is something your child can play with his friends. It will reassure him that his own opinion of what he thinks are his personal strengths is correct and it can reveal special qualities he never realised he had. Children with a low self-esteem can struggle to name good things about themselves which is why it's great if you or someone else can highlight their strengths for them. Maybe your child doesn't realise he is very good at organising things or very single-minded when it comes to getting things done. When this is pointed out it'll give him the confidence to volunteer to help the teacher at school or to put his name forward to be on the school council.

There is one drama game called Pretend You're An Object. This takes the onus off your child initially because he's not talking about himself. If he pretends to be a pair of shoes you can ask him about the shoes' qualities. He might say he makes children run faster or keeps a person's feet dry when it rains. If he pretends to be a pencil he might say he helps children to write neatly. After a while move the game onto talking about your child's own strengths. By now he should be able to name many good points about his personality, such as how he helps others, is friendly or is an excellent footballer. Remind him of all those splendid certificates on his bedroom wall.

If your child is finding it difficult to say what he excels at, create an imaginary 'scale-o-meter' in the room where one end is '100% positive', the middle is '50/50 average' and at the other end is 'unsure'. You can then ask him questions and see where on the scale-o-meter he runs to. Is he good at sport? Is he a good reader? If you make a note of how he rates each question you'll discover what he feels confident about in life so you can encourage him more in these areas. It is also great fun if you swap roles and other family members have a go on this pretend scale-o-meter. This will show your less-confident child how everyone has different interests and different qualities.

Try another idea...

Don't expect your child to make big improvements in her confidence overnight even if she's spending more time doing the things she is good at. Have a read through IDEA 38, *Confidence is a gradual process.*

Defining idea...

'Hide not your talents, they for use were made. What's a sun-dial in the shade?'
BENJAMIN FRANKLIN

How did it go?

Q **My son has always been a confident swimmer but since he went up a class and found things more difficult his confidence has disappeared. How can we get back his self-belief and enthusiasm?**

A *It is important to stress the reason he was put up a class was because the teacher thinks he is a superb swimmer. That's not changed. Get him to see the new class as a challenge and remind him how he has always been a stronger swimmer than many of his friends and maybe some children who are older than him. He needs to embrace this challenge as an actor would a difficult role given to him by a director convinced he has the ability to conquer it. You should also reward him when he makes progress in his new class.*

Q **Won't my son become a bit big-headed and arrogant if everyone keeps telling him he's such a good swimmer for his age?**

A *Reiterating his strengths as a good swimmer will not do him any harm, especially as his ego has taken a bit of a knock since he went up a class. However, you are right to make sure he doesn't become complacent and boastful. In the world of acting, people who seem to appear everywhere on television one minute can vanish without trace the next. The important thing is your son knows he's a good swimmer, continues to work hard so he gets even better and retains his confidence in his ability.*

29

Acting without judgement

There is no right or wrong in the theatre as actors learn to accept each other's opinions. Children can flourish too if they are in a non-judgemental environment.

Just think how boring and unrealistic your favourite soap opera would be if everyone looked like Brad Pitt or Cameron Diaz.

Directors need characters that reflect real life so whether you're fat, thin, bald, old or speak with a regional accent, there's a role for you somewhere. Many actors were teased as children about how they looked or behaved but they've grown in confidence through performing, helped by the applause and adulation that comes with being on stage. Some have even become unlikely sex symbols thanks to the roles they've taken on. This is not about turning the theatre into some kind of circus sideshow similar to those popular spectacles of the 19th century when bearded ladies topped the bill. We're pointing out that the acting profession is a good example of how children and adults can prosper because they're not judged by how they look.

Here's an idea for you...

Get your child to think about different parts of his body and then ask him about each bit. What makes his arms special? If he mimes a job he does with his arms can you guess what it is? He might say his arms are great for giving cuddles. What about his eyes or his mouth? Does he like to sing? This exercise highlights the use of the body rather than what it looks like. Actors must be very aware of how their bodies work and move.

If your child feels she's not fitting in or is being teased, she can gain in confidence by learning how standing out from the crowd rather than always blending in actually has its advantages.

It's also important she learns not to judge other people she meets simply because of the way they look, act or the things they say. Everyone's opinions are valid however much they might annoy her or however much she disagrees with them.

It can be hard for a child to accept he's different. Maybe he's taller for his age than all his friends and this is affecting his confidence? You can point out famous people who have done very nicely, thank-you, out of being tall – such as top basketball players Michael Jordan and Allen Iverson, who made millions of dollars by making their height work for them in a positive way. It's also a sure bet his friends will soon catch up with him.

Actors will write down everything good and bad about the character they're playing. This is an acting technique you can try at home to give your child's self-esteem a lift. Sit down with him and make an 'I am special' list where you note down everything that is special about your son. Maybe he has lovely bright blue eyes, is kind, good at maths, better than his friends at sport or brilliant at drawing? By pointing out the positive things people have mentioned about him in the past he'll feel much better about himself. Remind him that children often tease each other because they're jealous.

Actors respond in different ways to theatre critics and children too can be very sensitive to criticism. Check out IDEA 7, *Lovely darling, but ...*, for ways to tackle this.

Try another idea...

There is another drama game which families or after-school clubs can play to help children feel more secure. It goes like this. One child leaves the room and everyone else must list some positive things they thought about her when they first met her. They might mention how friendly she was, her smile or her trendy clothes. When the child returns she must try and guess who said which flattering remarks. This game is not designed to embarrass a child but to make her appreciate how highly she's thought of. It can also make her realise that children she did not regard as her friends actually really like her. Your child's confidence can also suffer if she's too shy or embarrassed to chat about what's bothering her.

Actors will always talk through different roles with the director to explain their worries and discuss their own limitations. Over time performers learn to live with and exploit any differences they were perhaps self-conscious about when they were kids. Their message to the audience today is 'This is how short, tall or fat I am so take me or leave me – I don't care.'

'*Even if we could observe all of a person's acts and words we would still not have sufficient information to judge him because we cannot see his reasons for his behaviour.*'
KENNETH L. HIGBEE, author

Defining idea...

How did it go?

Q **My son loves cubs and has attended for more than a year but recently he has been reluctant to go. It turns out some boys are teasing him about his weight. How can I convince him to ignore them?**

A *Make sure the scout leader is aware of the problem and how sensitive he is about it. Don't force him to go to cubs but if he doesn't attend point out to him how the group is missing his contribution. Boost his confidence by focusing on the positives. Maybe your son is one of the best at tying knots and teaching the other boys? The scout leader should be able to subtly put an end to the name-calling without drawing attention to your son.*

Q **But why does it always seem to be my child who is picked on?**

A *As a parent it can sometimes seem like that. Despite your concerns don't make your child aware you're so worried or you risk labelling him in the same way many actors get typecast. There are many performers who have been pigeon-holed because of the way they look or sound. You may actually be seeing a situation which in reality does not exist. Making a big deal about it won't help your child's confidence and will make him and you reluctant to try new things in life because you'll be so worried about him being picked on at any new group or club he attends.*

30

Sibling rivalries

Like an understudy waiting in the wings, what happens if one child lives in the shadow of a more confident sibling? Less self-assured children can thrive too with the right approach.

The Jacksons, the Osmonds and the Kennedys are just three famous families where some children are perceived as more successful than their brothers and sisters.

Where there are siblings you will always get comparisons. Think about it. If one son is great at sport and always being picked for various school teams it won't be long before questions are being asked about why his brother cannot run as fast or hit a ball quite so far. Such comments can be harsh and hurtful even if the people making them usually don't mean to be cruel. It can have a negative effect on a child's confidence because they feel inadequate.

In the world of theatre and television, brothers and sisters of famous actors can often feel over-shadowed by a celebrity sibling. They worry they're being perceived as less successful simply because they have normal jobs – and normal salaries – like the rest of us. Academics in the US reckon it's no surprise that a child responds

There is a great exercise called Identipicture. OK, that's a made-up name but it really gets a group of kids involved. Put everyone's name in a hat and ask each child to pick a name and describe the child they have chosen by their personality rather than their looks. They can only say positive things. Can the others guess in one minute who is the giggly one who hates spaghetti? This emphasises how children have different qualities to their siblings.

negatively if he's being compared to his siblings. Oh yes, and as an aside they also point out that children who are bored are more likely to start fights, but we digress.

There's a drama technique actors use to develop characters which, with a little adaptation, will help a shy child emerge from his brother's or sister's shadow. You'll need a pen and paper for this one which, in the absence of anything more creative, we've called Unique Description Cards. The idea is simple. Gather together a few of the family's children, both siblings and cousins, and ask them to write down two things about their appearance or personality that makes them different from everyone else in the room. Maybe they have different colour hair, longer legs or they seem to laugh all the time. You collect the cards, read out the comments and see if the children can guess who wrote what. This will highlight qualities in every child.

You can try these exercises too:

■ Next time your child has a birthday party play 'I Am Special Because …'. Kids stand in a circle and one at a time run in and shout out 'I am special because … (I can wiggle my ears)'. Less confident kids have a tendency to repeat what their older brother says, so you might want to give them something to shout by whispering in their ear.

- Whenever you play drama games, such as Charades, as a family make sure the less confident child goes first from time to time. If he's always following a brother who performs everything really well he can feel intimidated.

Inside the theatre and throughout the working world generally there'll always be accusations of nepotism.

One way to avoid sibling rivalry is to ensure all children are encouraged to excel at the specific things they're good at. Take a look at IDEA 28, *Tapping into your child's talents*, and you'll see what we mean.

Try another idea…

Many performers have faced charges of favouritism because they are related to someone famous. Let's face it, the power of the surname can certainly open doors. One would expect Nancy Sinatra found it much easier to at least get heard by record companies thanks to her superstar father Ol' Blue Eyes himself. Yet in most cases such queue-jumping will come to nothing unless a person is talented enough in their own right. And who can argue with the quality of Nancy's 60s hit 'These Boots Are Made for Walkin''?

Charges of nepotism are even thrown around in children's clubs and societies. If your child is being teased that she's only achieved something because of who her brother or sister happens to be, it can destroy her confidence. One way to avoid this is to encourage your kids to enjoy completely different hobbies. That way it's much more difficult for people to compare them.

'You don't choose your family. They are God's gift to you, as you are to them.'

DESMOND TUTU

Defining idea…

137

How did it go?

Q **One of our daughters has the talent to be on stage but her younger sister also wants to attend drama classes. Should I encourage her to do something different in her spare time?**

A *Some parents can pre-decide which of their children will be good at certain things. When it comes to drama we've seen parents arrive with precon- ceived ideas about which one of their kids will be the star and which one is just doing it as a hobby. This can put an enormous amount of pressure on the shoulders of the one ear-marked for greatness, whilst the other can find it hard to emerge from her sister's shadow. If you are not careful you might not notice your younger daughter's talent and she'll not fulfil her potential and get the confidence boost that will bring.*

Q **They both enjoy the classes but isn't it bad news to have sisters in the same class when one is obviously better than the other?**

A *It is a huge misconception that everyone in a group, whatever the hobby, wants a starring role. Even in professional theatre companies there are many performers who are more than happy to be in the 'ensemble'. You will find that your daughters gravitate towards different things within the class, which should hopefully eliminate any competition between them. In drama classes there are different aspect for children to enjoy, whether it's the warm-up games or the stage performance at the end of term. In sports teams, too, siblings can flourish by playing in different positions.*

31

All singing, all dancing

The clever use of music, dance and song sets the mood on stage and by utilising the performing arts your child can express herself in a fun and energetic way.

Whether it's singing in the shower or dancing to a cheesy pop video, the enthusiasm children show for music should be embraced to improve their confidence.

Today's actor must be an all-rounder. He must be prepared to perform in a serious Shakespearean play one week and sing and dance in a television commercial dressed as a packet of washing powder the next. An actor who can demonstrate he's more than a one-trick pony will also remain physically fit and looking good.

Dance can be a great introduction to the performing arts for shy children. The thought of speaking out loud in a drama class can terrify some kids, but dancing as part of a group is much less daunting. Many dance troupes perform at local festivals and the dancers at the back are as important to any routine as those at the front. It means your child will enjoy the confidence boost of being on stage and getting

Here's an idea for you… **Form a pretend pop group. Get the children to choose a name and some music and see if they can devise a dance routine. They will need some guidance, so tell them the dance must include a starting and an ending position as well as a jump or turn and maybe some wiggles. If the group is likely to argue get each child to come up with a couple of steps. Kids love to express themselves through choreography.**

applause without being in the spotlight. If you are anything like us you can't help but move some part of your body when you hear music, even if it's only the subtle tapping of a foot under the table. This is a perfectly natural response and different songs and tunes will inspire different feelings in your child. If she really likes a song from a particular television show or movie she will often learn the words and actions that go with it. Many pop bands deliberately keep their dance steps simple because they know their fans will want to copy them. If your child has learned the movements to a song she will feel less self-conscious about running onto the dance floor when she hears it being played at a party.

Everyone feels more confident exposing their dancing moves when a song is familiar. We've all seen the mums and dads (and grannies) rise together from their chairs at a wedding when the DJ puts on Little Eva's 'The Locomotion'.

Many of the techniques used by dance teachers in a beginner's class are linked to drama and you can try them at home. There is one exercise called Popstar Walk where the teacher asks a child about her favourite pop star and tells her to walk or skip across the room just like that performer. Sing-along DVDs where the words come up on the television are great for encouraging children to sing and dance as well as helping with their reading. One child we know memorised a Spanish song she loved so much and got a huge confidence boost by impressing her relatives on holiday in Barcelona. Many adults still remember the French lullaby 'Frère Jacques' (translated into English as 'Are You Sleeping?'), which they learned as kids.

There are many drama games involving music. One of our favourites is Musical Bumps, which is basically Musical Chairs without the chairs. When the music stops players must quickly sit on the floor. Or how about Musical Statues where the children dance around the room and pose like a statue when the music ends? Any child who moves before the song starts again is out. This is a useful game if your child finds it hard to stand still.

Singing in a round is also ideal for boosting concentration and confidence. A quick rendition of 'London's Burning' with everyone in the family singing individually or in pairs can be great fun, especially on laborious car journeys. Music grabs our emotions and memories around the throat and refuses to let go. Playing a tune that reminds your child of a happy moment in her life – maybe a holiday, birthday party or trip to the theatre – can be enough to cheer her up and can give her the confidence to tackle her nerves.

It helps if your child is confident moving around in her own skin. It is certainly worth reading IDEA 20, *Let's get physical*.

Try another idea...

'When children learn to dance they start to aspire to achieve something positive.'
SAMMY FONFÉ, choreographer

Defining idea...

How did
it go?

Q **My child sings at the top of her voice at home but is very shy about expressing herself around others. I feel she could be a star in the making so how can I get her to open up outside the house?**

A *She obviously has an interest in music even if she is quite reticent about showing it publicly. You need to develop this interest without pushing her too hard to perform in front of others. Why not see if she will join the school choir where she'll be singing in a group? This would be a fun outlet for her self-expression and as her confidence grows she might eventually be happy to perform to family and friends. Then you will see if she really does have star quality or just enjoys singing as a hobby.*

Q **She seems more interested in pop music than the hymns sung by the school choir. Should I encourage her to sing in the genre of music she really enjoys?**

A *We'd be surprised if the choir only sings hymns. From our experience school choirs nowadays perform a range of traditional and contemporary songs. You might want to check with the teacher. There are also karaoke pop CDs you can buy or download off the internet. These backing tracks are great fun to sing along to. As your child becomes more confident she'll be ready to give different genres of music a try, so don't give up on the school choir idea just yet.*

32

Knowing when to laugh or cry

Comedy and tragedy sit side by side in the theatre and children's self-esteem will rise if they learn not to take things too seriously and to share their different experiences, both good and bad.

If an actor is to make any serious money out of his trade he must be able to play comic roles as convincingly as those more sombre Oscar-winning parts involving misery and torment.

Laughter is said to be the best medicine when someone is feeling down. It can also be incredibly infectious, as anyone who has ever watched a show of television bloopers will testify. As soon as one person on the set begins to giggle it's not long before the entire crew is in stitches. When actors need their character to cry they will often think of a really sad memory to bring on the waterworks. This could be serious stuff, such as the death of a family member. If that doesn't work there's

Here's an idea for you...

There is a drama game called Sweaty Socks which will cheer up your child. Ask him to sit opposite you and tell him he cannot smile or laugh. You must then ask him questions, such as what is his favourite food or colour, and he must answer only with the words 'sweaty socks'. If he laughs he is out of the game.

always the fail-safe 'tear stick' but few actors want to go on stage smelling of onions.

Reflecting on a tragic or happy moment can help your child cope with a difficult situation which might be harming his confidence and stopping him from reaching his full potential. Crying can release built-up tension whilst laughing can make your child realise that what has happened to him is not the end of the world. One way to convey this is to share your own experiences. An actor will prepare for a happy or sad role by talking through incidents from her own life with the rest of the cast during rehearsals. In the same way you can reveal some of your own embarrassing moments from when you were young. Maybe you were the one who wet herself at a school camp and was horrified and devastated at the time but can laugh about it now. Your child will realise that everyone in his class and everyone in his family has had embarrassing things happen to them in their lives. We remind our kids of the time Uncle Brian's wig blew off outside the church during my cousin's wedding.

If you can talk about your own experiences when your child is sad about something, maybe the death of a pet or a friend moving away from the area, he'll see that you really do understand what he's going through. This will help him accept what has happened and feel confident enough to move on. One game you can play as a family is to talk through happy and sad events from one year or even five years ago. What can your child remember about those times, how was he feeling then and how does he feel now about what happened? He might have been nervous about starting school or worried about going into hospital for an operation. He can look back on those events and see how well he coped.

Kids need to be able to vent their frustrations when feeling sad or upset. Check out IDEA 23, *Keeping a lid on anger*, to help your child let off steam.

Try another idea…

Believe it or not, it is often harder for actors to laugh realistically on stage without sounding like a cackling old witch than it is to turn on the tears. A good drama technique to follow with your child is to get them to laugh for one minute, but without telling them anything funny. They will find this very difficult. When they have finished remind them of an incident they found hilarious and they should be able to laugh for one minute without any problem. Maybe your child remembers you banging into a door in front of other parents during a school visit or dropping Sunday lunch over the kitchen floor when you saw a huge spider on your arm. He will find it easier to laugh this time and will see how well you have managed to brush off situations you felt really awkward about when they happened.

'Comedy is tragedy plus time.'
CAROL BURNETT,
American actress and comedienne

Defining idea…

Such exercises are not designed to encourage your child to laugh at others' expense but to get her to accept that embarrassing and tragic things happen to everyone.

How did it go?

Q   Recalling my most embarrassing moments is all very well but my daughter tripped and fell walking into assembly last week and the whole school laughed at her. How can she get over something like that?

A   *We can try to analyse everything, particularly what happens to our children. Don't be frightened to bring up the subject of her fall in a light-hearted way because it is important she does not take what happened too seriously and worries about it for ages. If you don't want to bring up an anecdote of your own, make one up about someone else or recall one from a favourite film or television show. This should be the trigger that makes her see the funny side. There are probably also examples she can think about where someone else in her class fell over and was laughed at and how that has been forgotten.*

Q   One problem is that her brothers and sisters are teasing her horribly about it and have started to call her names for being clumsy. What should I do about that?

A   *Maybe she should try and accept that some people are clumsy in life and it is one of the quirkier sides to her character. Point out different traits in her brothers and sister and that we all have human flaws which we love in each other. People could be calling her far worse names. Actors cry out for such foibles in their personality as that can be what gets them noticed and wins them a role.*

33

Get that spider off me – facing phobias

An actor would overcome his arachnophobia rather than turn down a part in *Spider-Man*. Whatever your child's fears, discussing them and acting them out can put worries into perspective.

In the fiercely competitive world of the performing arts an actor cannot afford to let an irrational fear of anything lose him a job.

We know vegetarians who have eaten hot dogs to win roles in television commercials. This makes perfect sense if you think about it. If an actor is playing a tough nightclub bouncer who during a scene must eat greasy fast food while on duty outside a venue, then that's what he must eat. Watching him tuck into a rocket salad would not seem quite so real somehow. Many people have illogical fears that can spoil their enjoyment of life. A survey by those clever people at the National Institute of Mental Health in the US has discovered that more than 18% of Americans suffer from phobias. If we had any spare dollars we'd wager our very last one

If your child is scared of something, act out different scenarios. Maybe she hates needles but must have an injection? Share stories about injections you have had during your life. Then act out a scene where you are the nurse and your child keeps waving her arm around making things difficult. Then swap roles. This time you play the role of a friendly child who helps the nurse and gets a treat when everything is over. Go through the outcome of what will happen at the doctor's and talk through why the injection is important.

that some of these people are actors who have had to conquer their nightmares to win a part.

A child's confidence can take a severe dent if he has a specific dread of something. Perhaps it's the dark, insects, dogs, bees or flying that terrifies him. Such fears can stop a child from participating in activities and affect his education and social life. Social phobias can certainly make kids anxious in public. They can be constantly worried that others will judge them and will be reluctant to join in conversations just in case they say something silly. They'll also worry for ages about something they said or did.

Actors are told by their agents not to admit their phobias or mention any ethical preferences when auditioning. If they win a role and need to deal with something they are frightened of they'll usually introduce the subject into ice-breaking games before rehearsals start. Your child can address her phobias in the same way. One exercise is to have children sitting in a circle and one by one they must mention something that really makes them cringe. It could be snakes or blood. We know one child who cannot go near an orange without shivering uncontrollably. This exercise opens up phobias for discussion and children often end up laughing about their experiences and realise that, perhaps, there's not much to worry about after all.

If your child is too nervous to even talk about her fear then mime can be a useful drama technique to use. You can call the exercise Things That I Find Scary and play it when her friends come over. If we were playing this game we'd act out our reluctance to stand on the top of a high cliff or climb a tall tree to demonstrate our fear of heights. After all, if God had meant us to be that high he'd have given us wings, right? Other ideas:

Try another idea...

There will be many occasions when your child will have to confront his phobia without you around. Read up on how to help your child confront personal issues in IDEA 37, *The solo performance.*

- If your child screams at the sight of an insect, give the creature a name and some cute characteristics. How about Sydney the spider? You and your child can create a voice for Sydney and even make up a story.
- A fear of the dentist is quite common among young children. Act out beforehand what will happen and promise your child a reward afterwards.

Actors do use their own phobias in a positive way and children can too to build their confidence. If a performer is scared of heights this can actually help when playing someone hanging from the top of a building. A hatred of rats can come out if they're prisoners in a dungeon.

You can set scenes for your child and her friends to act out to help them overcome their particular fears. This will help them understand that most phobias are irrational and the things they're scared of won't actually harm them.

Defining idea...

'Remember that fear always lurks behind perfectionism. Confronting your fears and allowing yourself the right to be human can, paradoxically, make you a far happier and more productive person.'
DR DAVID M. BURNS, author of *The Feeling Good Handbook*

149

How did
it go? **Q** **My daughter is really uncomfortable when she must have physical contact with other children at school. She hates holding hands with her classmates. How can we overcome that?**

A *Some physical drama games can break down mental obstructions which have created phobias. One which comes to mind is when two people stand opposite each other. Your daughter can play this with a sibling first and then with her school friends. The object is to touch the other person behind the back of their knees. The first person with five taps is the winner. This game removes barriers and gets kids exercising in a fun way.*

Q **Halloween celebrations really freak out my son, who is scared of ghosts and witches. How can I get him to realise these characters are not real?**

A *Try exploring ghosts in a pleasurable way. Watch some DVDs featuring nice characters such as* Casper the Friendly Ghost *or* Sabrina, The Teenage Witch. *This will show him how ghosts are all about entertainment. Spooks and ghouls are in his imagination so you need to help him bring them to life is a positive way. He could write his own friendly ghost story and draw some illustrations.*

34

New friends, new situations

Actors bond quickly as they face a race against time to rehearse and put on a show. Encouraging your child to widen his own social circle will do wonders for his self-confidence.

Believe it or not actors get very nervous before the first rehearsal. Many will spend ages deciding what to wear to impress the rest of the cast at the first meeting.

As in life generally, first impressions count massively in the theatre where an actor will move from job to job, working with hundreds of different people throughout her career. This means most actors, even the shy ones, become extremely confident in social situations because they know it can take a real effort to make new friends. Imagine being thrown together with a group of performers on the good ship Actors' Ego for a two-month cruise around the Mediterranean? The occasional tantrum is expected, but life is so much more bearable if everyone gets along. A cabaret singer who feels like throwing herself overboard every evening because of dressing room bitchiness is bad news for everyone's morale. When actors begin working on a play the director will initiate different physical and mental exercises to break the

A fun exercise is called Celebrity Party. Make one child host the party while the other children or family members must be someone famous that everyone else would know. They must think about how that person would walk and speak. When they enter the party the host must guess who they are by asking questions such as where do they live or what do they do all day? This is good practice for children who can feel nervous venturing into new social situations.

ice. She might ask each person to say something funny about themselves.

Children will grow in confidence too if they get used to mixing with different kids in different situations. Widening your child's social circle can seem a difficult task because every kid has his best friends and can be quite stubborn about who he plays with. Try inviting children for tea who he knows but who perhaps he's not formed strong relationships with. These might be kids his age who live in your street or cousins he's not very close to. This can take a lot of effort but the rewards in terms of confidence can be rich. Any awkwardness when these new kids arrive can be quickly removed with a few acting games.

- Get the kids to sit on the floor opposite one another and ask them to discover five things about the other person. This usually prompts some really interesting conversations and hopefully the children will realise they have plenty in common.
- Try a round of The Complainer. This is a good game to introduce once your child and his guests have started to play together. One of them pretends to be on the phone in a shop and the other must come in and make it difficult for them to continue their conversation by complaining. You can suggest the

first line they must say such as 'I want my money back', and they take it from there. You can expect to hear plenty of giggles when you feel ready to leave them alone to play.

If your child is shy about approaching other children at a party you can point out another guest who is perhaps the same age or wearing the same colour clothes and introduce them to each other. Finding simple common ground like this can be all kids need to start playing together and form new friendships.

Another suggestion is to invite kids from a club your child belongs to, maybe a dance troupe or a football or chess team, to practise at your house. Your child's confidence will also be boosted if he becomes used to talking to other responsible adults. You could introduce him to your own friends during your work or leisure time so he feels comfortable in different situations or when he has to visit the doctor or dentist. He'll be more confident in different social and professional environments as he gets older because he'll be used to mixing with a variety of people, of varying ages and backgrounds. And you can never have too many friends.

Kids who step out of their comfort zone occasionally can widen their network of friends. Check out IDEA 41, *Daring to be different*, to see how this can work.

Try another idea…

'Make new friends and keep the old, one is silver and the other gold.'
The Girl Scouts' motto

Defining idea…

How did
it go?

Q **After school my child goes to a child minder who looks after two other children who are very good friends. My daughter often feels left out. What can she do to feel more involved?**

A *Next time you collect your daughter, ask her about the other girls to show you're interested. Help her find things that all three of them have in common. You're effectively putting ideas into your child's head. You could also suggest a game she can play with the other two girls. Here's one called Waiting At The Bus Stop. One child chooses to be a character, maybe a mum, tramp, posh lady or a school child. The next girl joins the bus stop as a different character and starts a conversation. Then one sits down and the third girl approaches. They could be stereotypical characters like old people moaning about kids on the bus or the teenager playing loud music. This is a great game when you have three children which, as we all know, can be a tricky number.*

Q **What if my daughter doesn't have the confidence to suggest a game?**

A *If you practise at home with her siblings or friends we're sure she'll want to suggest a round of Waiting At The Bus Stop. The alternative is to invite the two girls from the child minder for tea at yours one day. If you do this, invite one of your daughter's close friends too so nobody feels left out. The bus stop game works just as well with four.*

35

Let me entertain you – whatever the job!

Even if an actor hates a play it's his job to keep the audience entertained. If your child won't pull her weight around the house, try making boring tasks fun.

No child likes tidying his room or doing chores, yet kids can get a boost from contributing more to the running of the home. Honestly, it's true!

If your child's reading this she might think there's some kind of parental conspiracy going on to re-instate child labour. That's not on the agenda just yet, but there are some interesting bits of information floating about which demonstrate how everyone benefits if kids help around the house. A study by boffins at the University of Minnesota has discovered that people who did chores when they were as young as four were more successful and confident adults. These helpful Harrys did better at school, completed their education and got a good start in their career. It even had an impact on whether they took drugs. Now you're listening.

Here's an idea for you... **If your child has an English project for his homework – maybe he must review a book – try to do something different like create a newspaper front page. He could play the role of a reporter and investigate the big stories within the plot. His teacher will love it.**

Of course, we'd all love it if children would help out more with simple tasks, such as room tidying, taking out the rubbish or helping to weed the garden. One of the reasons they are so reluctant is actually staring us right in the face. Most of these jobs are mind-numbingly dull. When actors get bored with doing the same piece night after night they yearn for something out of the ordinary to happen to get them excited again. Whether it's in the workplace or at home, once the words 'routine' and 'boring' become interchangeable the alarm bells should start ringing, and loudly. So how do you make boring tasks fun so kids will want to do them? If an actor is finding it hard to get excited about a role or a long monologue, the director will tell him to try to relate the character's troubles and needs to his own personality. He is basically asking the actor to find something – anything – within the piece which interests him so he becomes enthused.

Now adapt this idea within your own four walls to get your daughter to tidy her bedroom which looks like a chemistry lesson gone wrong. Give her an end goal to aim for. Tell her you will mark the room's tidiness out of 10. If she gets less than five she cannot go out and play but if she scores more than five she can. Notch up a perfect 10 and it's burgers for supper. If your daughter is younger but equally as unenthusiastic, let her pretend to be Cinderella sent to her room to clean it. She could dress in costume and you could play the evil stepmother or ugly sister going up to her room every few minutes. Remind her that Cinders got her reward in the end.

Here are some other ideas:

- If your child lacks enthusiasm for her homework, play a game of schools. You can be the teacher who helps and encourages her. You can give her the confidence to try something different in the same way actors take risks with characters to make them more interesting. Rather than just drawing trees like the other kids in her class she could collect leaves from the park to stick in her book.

- If you want your child to help prepare Sunday lunch, turn the whole process into a pretend cookery programme.

- Don't just ask her to help you in the garden, give her a 'role' of her own in making it a success. She could have her own small plot to grow whatever she likes. Weeding may be a chore but growing your own vegetables is inspiring and rewarding. When they appear on the table her pride and confidence will get a huge lift.

By making boring tasks entertaining, the work gets done without the raised voices, blazing rows and subsequent headaches that can come with them.

You often need to be creative to make tasks fun. There are some tips on this in IDEA 39, *It's just my imagination*.

Try another idea…

'If you really want to succeed, you'll have to go for it every day like I do. The big time isn't for slackers. Keep up your mental stamina and remain curious. I think bored people are unintelligent people.'
DONALD TRUMP

Defining idea…

How did it go?

Q **My daughter goes to a homework club after school and is under the strict supervision of the teacher. How can I get her to think of the club as fun and not just as extended school hours?**

A *You can still give your daughter inspirational ideas even if you aren't around when she's actually given and does her homework. Just spend some time finding out about the projects she's working on and give her some creative ideas to take with her to the homework club. If she's studying Ancient Egypt why not help her to collect information which she can share with her friends and the teacher to inspire everyone in the class? A good actor will spend time preparing for a show by researching the story and characters and during rehearsals will try different ways of doing things. Good ideas will be taken up by the rest of your daughter's class, which will be great for her confidence.*

Q **What if she doesn't have the confidence to make suggestions to the whole homework club?**

A *If you've thought up some good ideas at home, make sure you write them down and put them in a little folder she can take to the teacher. Teachers love showing examples to the rest of the class and any words of encouragement will convince your daughter it is worth coming up with creative suggestions again and again.*

36

Lights, camera, action

The theatre needs the right equipment to function. Just think of the imagination-triggering fun your child can have with cameras, lights and a microphone.

It's a common misconception that techies in theatre and TV are desperate to get in front of the camera.

Contrary to popular belief the lighting operators, cameramen and members of the sound team are happy enough with their own role in making a show a success. That includes the person in TV who holds that fluffy microphone on a stick – the boom operator. As an odd aside it's amazing how many actors and dancers end up marrying a techie. When they visit the theatre together one is watching the show while the other spends more time checking out the speakers on the wall and the lighting rig.

Even the shabbiest set constructed from bits and pieces bought cheaply through online auction sites can come to life thanks to creative lighting. Old musty costumes will look exquisite once the lighting experts wield their magic. All a far cry from Shakespeare's time when plays had to be performed in the afternoon before it got dark.

Here's an idea for you...

Next time you have a family party let your child pretend to be a presenter from the hit reality show, *Big Brother*. Instead of having them wandering around the house hassling guests, create a Diary Room in a quiet corner. Ask an older sibling or cousin to be the cameraman using a camcorder while your child fires questions at the guests in the 'room'. 'So what has been the nicest thing about the afternoon?' or 'Is there any message you want to leave the anniversary couple?' The end result can be played to the guests later.

Kids are used to playing with technical gadgets and gizmos these days. In fact, they're usually more comfortable on a computer or programming their television to record programmes than their parents. Such superiority can be its own confidence booster. Technical equipment can activate your child's imagination and encourage him to delve deep into his creativity.

Simple things like using a cheap voice recorder can help his speech development. He and his friends can make their own radio show or he could keep a verbal diary when he's away from home. These devices will tell you whether your child talks too fast or slow, or too quietly. He'll become more confident as he learns to adjust his speech.

Many families have a camcorder and if you trust your child to use yours without breaking it there's plenty of creative fun to be had. The kids could make a documentary about an issue they feel strongly about. Here's some quick cameraman advice from our man behind the lens, Gary. He tells amateurs filming anything, even holiday videos, to always change the picture angle and use the zoom sparingly to make the finished product that much more interesting. Don't forget to add a voice over and some music. A camcorder is also an excellent tool for helping kids rehearse their dance steps or practice their football skills. Kids (and adults) can always have fun with a microphone whether it's real or not. For microphone think hairbrush-in-front-of-the-mirror.

Buying a karaoke machine or just a sing-along DVD can really encourage your child to be more adventurous with his speech and movements. He could also pretend to be a television presenter who interviews his friend who's a celebrity. You could even record the interview on the voice recorder or camcorder. The possibilities are endless.

Try another idea...

Your child may be more technically minded than you realise. IDEA 28, *Tapping into your child's talents*, gives some helpful tips on encouraging kids in the things they're good at.

Defining idea...

'With technology in the theatre you need an ability to maintain concentration. You have to stay focused and not panic or one mistake can turn into a string of errors.'
STUART MOFFAT, sound engineer in London's West End

We all know great lighting can bring theatre to life so why not turn off all the lights and use a camping lantern or torch to create a fantastic story-telling atmosphere at home? Careful use of lighting can help children calm down after a busy day and improve their confidence in the dark. Next time you have a birthday or Halloween party, dust off those Christmas lights from the attic or change the colour of the bulbs around the house to create the atmosphere you want.

Musical equipment is also crucial in the theatre. Basic instruments can be made to generate sound effects. Your child could make drums out of empty ice cream tubs or chimes from milk bottles filled to different levels with water.

Whoever said a techie's life was dull?

Q   **My daughter always ends up doing the behind-the-scenes roles in the school productions, helping with sound effects and the music, rather than performing. Why can't she be given the chance to be the leading lady?**

How did it go?

A   *In most school productions children tend to choose what role or job they want to do. Perhaps she asked to be in the music department because that's what she enjoys and where she feels the most confident? She's still part of the team involved in making the production a success. It can be a mistake to assume everyone wants to be on stage and the centre of attention. Think about what the show would be missing if there was no music or were no sound effects. Your daughter's job is vital.*

Q   **That's all very well but my husband and I still have to go and watch these shows and we don't get to even see her. Should we stay away?**

A   *It is important you take an interest so you're aware what your child is doing in the show. If she is in charge of the sound, listen out for specifics which you can talk to her about later. This will really help her confidence and make her realise how important she is to the production. If she tells you she'd like to be one of the actors next time then help her to pluck up the courage to ask the teachers when the casting takes place.*

37

The solo performance

Children must learn how to confront personal issues on their own. Like an actor mastering a monologue, if your child has the confidence to go it alone her self-belief will rocket.

Whether it's carrying a piano up the stairs or standing in front of people and reading a poem, it's a lot harder when no one's there to help you.

When one of his lead actors missed his cue because he was still in the toilet, a famous West End theatre producer instinctively pushed one of his ensemble actors on stage and told him to 'fill the time, babe'. The poor man ended up with a 10-minute slot which he managed to complete superbly by chatting with the audience and asking them to vote for which part of the show they've liked the best so far. His first-ever solo role was a massive success.

Any actor performing alone must have enough confidence in his ability to hold the audience's attention. He also needs enough self-belief not to be fazed by the occasional critical comment about his performance. It can be extremely nerve-wracking for your child to do things on her own. Yet it's also a natural step on the long

Here's an idea for you...

The next time your child is going on a trip without you, make her prepare early to grow in confidence. What clothes or cuddly toys will she take? You can sprinkle some magic 'make me brave' fairy dust over everything. Why not get your child to write a thank-you letter in advance? As much as possible let your child make her own plans so she feels independent and mentally prepared to fly solo.

journey towards independence. The first time she puts up her hand in class or volunteers for something takes guts. She might have to read a piece of text in assembly or in church, cope with the very important role of Mary in the school nativity play or perform a solo in her dance class's end of term show. When everyone's eyes are upon her, she'll sink or swim by how confident and prepared she is. It will affect the volume and clarity of her voice and whether she even remembers her lines or dance steps. She'll progress wonderfully if she's not afraid to walk up to the teacher to ask for something to be explained again or is happy to represent her class alone. She'll also feel more independent and confident if she can deal with difficult situations rather than relying on her parents marching in on her behalf with steam gushing from their ears.

An actor will rehearse for hours and your child can overcome her nerves by practising what she needs to do again and again. Why not video her dance routine or record her reading the passage she must recite in the school service?

By all means point out areas for improvement, but make sure you reiterate how good she already is to ensure her confidence doesn't drain away. Once she feels secure enough to fly solo all you need to give is love and support. Practice really does make perfect and the rewards your child gets from doing things on her own – just remind her about that swimming certificate on her wall or the badge she got from Brownies – will make her feel really proud. There's one exercise actors use to help them feel more comfortable when they must work alone. Ask your child and a friend to take it in turns sitting on a chair for a couple of minutes and, well, just sit there! Do nothing, zilch. Believe it or not, sitting in a chair and not doing anything is harder than it sounds. Just remember that next time you're bored at work. When the time is up get them to try it again. Now give them a reason for being there. Maybe they're waiting for a bus or for a friend who's late. This highlights to them how people can feel more comfortable and confident in a space on their own if they have something to think about.

If your child really focuses on the words she has to read or how her dance routine goes beforehand it should remove at least some of the nerves. Remember, though, a few butterflies in the tummy are essential to get the adrenaline pumping.

Try another idea…

Parents who try to push their children into solo roles in life can do more harm than good if they're not ready. IDEA 21, *You're not helping, Mum,* **highlights some of the warning signs.**

Defining idea…

'*You gain strength, courage and confidence by every experience in which you really stop to look fear in the face. You must do the thing which you think you cannot do.*'
ELEANOR ROOSEVELT

How did it go?

Q **My oldest daughter is getting married and wants her younger sister to read in church. She won't do it because she thinks nerves will make her fluff her lines on the big day. How can I encourage her?**

A *The worst thing you can do is put too much pressure on her. Tell her if she doesn't want to do it that's fine and you'll find someone else. Don't give up, though. It might be the words that are putting her off. Maybe it is beyond her reading ability for her age? Perhaps if you find a more suitable verse she'll have the confidence to do such a wonderful thing for her sister. She can also learn the piece like an actor would by marking on the paper where she should breathe and practising projecting her voice.*

Q **I think it's the thought of standing up in a church that's the big stumbling block. How can we overcome this as we cannot move the wedding venue?**

A *If she's scared of reading in a big church you could visit the place a couple of times and rehearse the piece. We're sure the vicar won't mind. Alternatively, you could suggest she reads at the reception later in the day. If all else fails she could write her own special poem and put it in a nice card for the bride and groom.*

38

Confidence is a gradual process

Actors train for years and never win the best parts straightaway. They set themselves attainable goals so don't expect your child to be the most confident kid in the street overnight.

Even the longest journey starts with one small step so please don't push your child too fast too early, or his confidence could crumble.

A few years ago an agent insisted an actor friend went along to Pineapple Studios in London to audition for the West End musical, *Chicago*. This is the show famous for some of the best dance routines in the world. No pressure then. To say the whole audition was a complete disaster would be an understatement. Her dancing just didn't crack it on the day and her confidence went south. Looking back on this embarrassing moment it seems the agent was being far too ambitious on her client's behalf. Let's just say the girl took a lot of persuading before she attended another musical theatre audition.

Here's an idea for you... **To really assess how much more confident your child has become, look backwards. Does she remember how nervous she was during her first day at school? What were her worries and what friends does she have now that she didn't before? Discuss the high points at school, such as the certificates and stickers she has won. Can she give an imaginary child some advice for when they're feeling nervous?**

There is a lesson for all of us here. When we see talent in our kids and feel tempted to drive them that little bit too hard just stop and think about the possible impact on their confidence. What's that old saying about not running before you can walk? If you expect to see significant progress in your child's confidence straightaway you could fail to notice small, but very important, gradual improvements. Your child might not be getting solo pieces during the class assembly but at least she's more confident and comfortable standing at the front with his classmates. A few months ago the thought of doing even that would have driven her back to the safety of her duvet.

We know one kid who was too scared to even talk out loud in class before he joined a drama club. After two terms of acting exercises he was happy to take part in class performances. After a whole year he was ready to go on stage. His mum was extremely patient and willing to persevere. She now reports how his confidence in all subjects at school has increased considerably.

There are many drama exercises which can help to reinforce the positive strides your child makes over a short period of time. Sit down with him and write his biography as if it were an actor's life story to be published in a programme for a theatre production. List all his successes and accomplishments so his siblings, friends and family know how great he is and how much progress he's made. You could go a step further and create a web page complete with a photo of your child alongside a list of his positive traits and triumphs to highlight his personal development. There is one great acting game which will help your child gradually build up his confidence. It's called Number Talk and actors use it to explore colour and tone in their voices.

Any improvement in a child's self-esteem can be held back if they feel over-shadowed by a really confident sibling. IDEA 30, *Sibling rivalries*, explains how to avoid this.

Try another idea...

Ask your child and a friend to think up a very short conversation that might take place between two characters. An argument is particularly fun. How about a mother telling off her son for having bad table manners? The children must act out the scene but can only talk in numbers. Sounds strange we know, but they can choose any number they like. Perhaps the angrier they get the higher the number they use? Anyone watching this fascinating story unfold will still understand the general gist of what's going on by the tone and volume of the children's voices. This game is perfect for shy kids nervous about speaking out loud in front of other children. By focusing on numbers they don't have to worry about what words are passing their lips. After a few weeks of playing Number Talk you'll know when you child is confident enough to turn the numbers into words.

'Success is a journey not a destination. The doing is usually more important than the outcome. Not everyone can be number one.'
ARTHUR ASHE, tennis legend.

Defining idea...

How did it go?

Q **My son has attended an after-school club for months but still cries when we arrive and has to be taken into the room by the teacher. Why is it such hard work to get him there?**

A *Whatever you do, don't give up! He might have developed the crying at the start of the club as a habit. When this happens at drama classes the best thing to do is to drop him off quickly and leave without making too much of a fuss. Some children we know cry every time they arrive for a whole term but a year on they're positively rushing to get through the door into the class.*

Q **My other concern is the end of term show, which parents are encouraged to watch. My son says he won't perform if I'm in the audience. Should I stay away so he still benefits from taking part?**

A *This problem is more common than you think. It's probably best that on this occasion you do stay away so he gets all the confidence benefits of being on stage and receiving applause. Afterwards ask him to tell you all about it in graphic detail, and you will probably find he wishes you had seen it. The boost he got from performing should mean he's eager to have you in the audience next time. But don't make too much of a fuss if not. Slow but steady is the name of the game when helping any child gain in confidence.*

39

It's just my imagination

The imagination is an actor's deadliest weapon. The importance of developing a creative imagination in your child should not be underestimated as she reveals talents she never knew she had.

If you've seen Andrew Lloyd Webber's hit musical *Starlight Express* you'd have completely believed the dining, smoking and buffet steam trains played by actors were competing in a race.

To bring such a story to life actors require vivid imaginations. As the audience, we may be sitting in a theatre, but if the story is set, say, on a desert island, we want to be transported there. The scenery can only do so much. A good actor will help us to imagine what the sea and air smells like, what sounds are around and how it feels emotionally to be stranded with little help of ever being rescued. Children also have vivid imaginations, enhanced by the books they read and the games they play. It is only as they get older that such inventiveness can become somewhat stilted because, as adults, we're all encouraged to conform. Boo hiss to that.

Here's an idea for you... **Ask your child to lie on the floor on her stomach and cup her face in her hands. By keeping her eyes closed she must imagine she is looking up into space from a rocket. What can she see? Ask her not to tell you straightaway but to really focus on the stars and planets and what it looks and even smells like. This exercise is ideal when children are over-excited and need some encouragement to calm down.**

Actors, on the other hand, continue to exploit their imaginations whatever their age because they must be ready for any role thrown their way. If your child is encouraged to use her imagination as much as possible it can make even the most mundane tasks enjoyable and magical. She'll also think more creatively at school in every subject, not just English. It'll give her bundles of confidence to contribute to class discussions. Most of our homes are stuffed full of electronic toys, but often children get more satisfaction from group games where they need to be creative and are actually involved in the action. This could be a game of shops, schools or a pretend battle with aliens from another planet.

There are plenty of drama exercises that get kids' imaginations working overtime. Try giving them the title of a story from which they must devise a short play. A good example would be 'The Haunted House'.

Kids become very excited when they're asked to create their own tale and parents can be amazed by some of the fantastic ideas they come up with. Every child's imagination is different so there might be a few arguments if the children have conflicting but equally valid ideas. As long as you supervise, everyone should be able to contribute something. This is, after all, all about working as a team as well as learning to negotiate. We mustn't forget that any form of role play is also great for improving kids' confidence in social situations.

Younger children can sometimes respond to requests to do things if we tap into their imagination. Your child might have a doll called Sally Ann. You can tell her that Sally Ann has asked her to stand straight or speak up. You can ask the doll what she thinks about different ideas and behaviour by holding her to your ear as though she's whispering to you. Your child will be captivated because you're bringing fantasy to life and she'll want to work hard to please her doll. Such use of toys as characters can be enough to set her imagination racing.

Another exercise is to get kids to think up a brand new cartoon character. What's its name? What type of character is it? Good or bad? What do they wear? Where do they live? How do they speak and move? The great thing about this game is that shy children will want to get involved because there are no right or wrong answers. They might even have the confidence to act out being their invented character. What happens when they meet one of their friends' creations? Don't forget to dust off your own creative mind by joining in any role play. You might actually enjoy it. Imagine that!

Try another idea...

Imagination games come easier if you have some tools to help you and a box of costumes and props is an obvious place to start. IDEA 11, *Dressing the part, make-up and all* and IDEA 4, *Prop till you drop*, both delve into this in more detail.

Defining idea...

'Imagination is more important than knowledge. Knowledge is limited. Imagination encircles the world.'

ALBERT EINSTEIN

How did it go?

Q **My son seems to spend his whole life locked in his own little world pretending to be one superhero or another. How can I get him to be himself more in family situations and talk to everyone?**

A *The fact your son has such a vibrant imagination is fantastic. One way to communicate with him is to take more of an interest in the characters he's creating. Get him to tell you and other members of the family about them and why they can save the world. He'll probably enjoy the attention and be happy to elaborate. It could spark a family discussion which he's more than happy to join in.*

Q **That's all very well, but my two daughters are too old to talk about superheroes and find the whole thing irritating. Shouldn't this be something I do with him alone?**

A *Your daughters may feel they're too old for some superheroes but you can still get conversations going around the dinner table by talking more generally. You could ask all your children who else on the planet they would like to be. Your son might say a superhero but your oldest daughter might want to be the Queen. What would they do differently if they could change places with that person for a week? Actors are always being set tasks like this when they're training because it encourages them to get their creative fluids surging.*

40

Have you read the script?

Many plays fail because of poor writing. Encouraging your child to pen a story with inspired characters and plot lines can make him a more confident reader and writer.

A production must hold our interest. The action must be stimulating and the characters real which is why the plot is so, so crucial.

During Shakespeare's time most playwrights wrote about social issues of the day. The plays were a fascinating commentary on life in Elizabethan England. They were the television soap operas of their day. It is a sure bet that the Gunpowder Plot in Britain in 1605, when barrels of explosives were smuggled into the British Parliament in a failed attempt to assassinate the king, was the inspiration for *Macbeth*. Of course, please refer to this as 'The Scottish Play' if you're reading this inside a theatre or legend has it you'll be cursed. Charles Dickens' classic tales tell us plenty about Victorian values, clothes and standards that have gradually disappeared over the last hundred years or so.

Writing things down can be a great way for your child to get problems off her chest and to express herself, especially if she's quite shy. During their training actors will

Here's an idea for you... **Hopefully your child will like writing stories. Get her to write a short script entitled 'My Life'. Who will be the main characters and where will it be set? Encourage her to focus around one special incident in her life, maybe a particular birthday or family holiday. If your child is too young to write it herself, she could always dictate it to you while you bash away on the computer. Actors have a 'read through' before starting rehearsals. Let the family read the script, playing out their own roles or someone else's.**

improvise scenes and this is a good place to start to get kids interested in writing. Be careful when you're encouraging your child and her friends to create a story that you're not too ambitious. Just make sure it has a beginning, middle and an end.

It can help if you give them some ideas to work with. Scene One: Gemma is on her way to school but doesn't want to go. Scene Two: At School. A new girl starts and she and Gemma make friends. Scene Three: Home time. Gemma comes bounding out of school and tells her mum she's made a new friend. This is a simple idea that kids can explore and then create uncomplicated dialogue around. It is certainly easier to write things down if you know how a story will start and finish.

Once the children have their basic idea they can begin to add different characters. What funny personalities can they introduce? What odd quirks do the people in the story have which the kids can add to their own performances? If your child went straight to trying to write lines for her characters without this verbal approach she'd probably spend ages staring at a blank piece of paper and soon get bored. By acting out a story first the ideas are already in your child's head when she actually comes to put pen to paper. This technique also helps her to explore appropriate vocabulary, which will boost her self-expression. Finishing a script is a huge confidence booster for kids because the end result is all their own work. They also feel a great sense of achievement when they see the reaction of others when they perform their play.

Words and pictures are natural partners so why not introduce some real-life images to a written story? IDEA 52, *Smile for the camera, please*, gives some helpful hints on how to make a visual impact.

Try another idea…

If your child is too young to write a script she can still be involved in the story telling and planning. In the business world this is called brainstorming. You could get each child to write single words on a piece of paper to fuel a discussion as their imaginations combine to create the theme of the play or a specific character. Don't forget to think about what props and costumes they might need. This exercise can go beyond being simply a script. The children can work together to turn it into a storybook. They could write one chapter each over time, illustrate it and even publish it via their computer printer and sell their novel to their parents.

These types of creative projects can also be a great way to bring a school topic to life. Your child will get praise from the teacher as well as enhancing her literacy skills in a really fun and fulfilling way.

'My aim is to put down on paper what I see and what I feel in the best and simplest way.'

ERNEST HEMINGWAY

Defining idea…

How did it go?

Q **I understand the benefits of writing but my child is only six years old. Surely that's too young to be writing scripts or stories?**

A *The knack is to grab children's interest when they're young. Why don't you and your child write a brand new fairytale together? She could come up with the names of the characters and describe to you what they look like and can even make up funny voices to show you how the different people sound. You can type out the story and see the look of pride on her face when her story is read by or to her friends and family. Put the story somewhere safe because it will become a very precious childhood memory.*

Q **How will my child be able to perform her finished masterpiece if she can't read?**

A *You can ask her to learn some lines from her story or script. This is a great way to boost her memory and her imagination. You can also spend plenty of time dressing her up as the lead character. She'll be very keen to recite her lines if she looks the part. Maybe she could invite some of her best friends to dress up and learn a couple of lines too?*

41

Daring to be different

Theatre experts believe it's better if actors take risks on stage rather than play it safe. Teaching your child to challenge herself by doing something daring occasionally will remove her inhibitions.

Actors who stand out from the crowd because they can play the guitar, ride a horse, have bright red hair or are seven feet tall will always get work.

Let's face it; most of us are pretty bog-standard. We might have the odd party trick to impress our friends, but when push comes to shove we're as good or bad as the next guy. In the theatre this is not always enough. Casting directors become bored seeing actor after actor read the same piece of audition script in the same style. They can be crying out for someone to come in and just try something different.

Here's an idea for you... **Next time you're out with your child tell him you're both going to do something daring and the reward will be a meal out. Choose something for your child which you know he can achieve. He could go up to a shop assistant and ask where the book section is or pay for something on his own. Stick to your end of the bargain too. You might have to try on a disgusting outfit in a clothes shop. Don't forget to take pictures!**

We recall one actor who was desperate to play baddy roles but was always being told he just looks too nice (a great problem to have if you are a used-car salesman, mind). Eventually he decided to do something about it. While on the train travelling to yet another audition to play a gangster he disappeared into the toilets. He put his wife's mascara on the underside of his face and smeared it around to look like stubble, darkened his eyebrows and changed into a black suit. He was met with some odd stares when he returned to his seat but he got the part.

It can be difficult for shy children to stand out from the crowd. It's far easier for them to blend in and go unnoticed. However, if you can encourage your child to take a chance by daring to be different his world could open up. If a risk goes well he'll be praised and encouraged for his efforts. Even if it doesn't go to plan he should receive acknowledgement for trying something out of the ordinary. It'll show his teacher he has the potential to be a leader and his confidence will get an additional boost if he's chosen to head a task or team.

There are some great exercises to help your child think for herself and to not just follow her friends. Next time she's playing with her pals get them each to think of a famous character they'd love to be. They're not allowed to choose the same person. They must then imagine they're at one of the character's houses and competing to win a part in a television series. Only one of them can win, so they must demonstrate their individual talents and skills. You can be the judge. The talents could be silly, funny or eyebrow-raisingly impressive. This game lets children take risks under the guise of being someone else. It will highlight how to be noticed you often need to catch the attention of the people who matter.

You can try a similar exercise when your child attends a fancy dress party. For Halloween you could encourage her not to be your standard witch but to be an evil sorceress. It creates more exciting costume and make-up opportunities to impress her friends. It is differences such as these which create the right kind of attention for your child. She'll be noticed by those around her as someone who always makes an effort, thinks beyond the obvious and wants to try new things.

Once your child is confident about being noticed he'll be better placed to cope with situations on his own. IDEA 37, *The solo performance*, has more advice on this scary prospect.

Try another idea…

'In order to be irreplaceable one must always be different.'
COCO CHANEL

Defining idea…

183

Another great acting game is Don't Tell Anyone But. Have a discussion with your child and her friends about how everyone is different and get each person to think of something about them which the others might think is slightly odd. Maybe they actually like cabbage or enjoy maths? After five minutes of thinking time each child must divulge their secret. The rule of the game is that everyone must agree to keep each person's revelation a secret. This game builds up trust and companionship as well as helping kids to realise we all have something which sets us apart from the crowd.

Q   **There's a school talent show coming up which my daughter has been asked to take part in. She's a good dancer but the thought of performing on her own on stage fills her with dread. How can I encourage her?**   *How did it go?*

A   *This is a great opportunity to build your child's confidence and get her noticed. The secret is not to expect her to perform anything too ambitious. Don't ask her to do a dance which she might get frustrated with when rehearsing at home before the competition. Maybe dancing is not the right thing for her first show? Perhaps it would be better if she read a poem she's written?*

Q   **With a little reassurance I think she'd like to dance, but she would feel more confident dancing with some friends. Would they be expected to choreograph their own routine?**

A   *It's more important your daughter and her friends perform something entertaining and which they feel confident about. They could copy a routine from a favourite pop video and dance to the song on stage. They could add to their act by creating costumes to look like the famous singers they are imitating. If they do have time to choreograph something keep it simple. They could be cheerleaders. Again, there are some great costume opportunities here. Remember having an imaginative costume is one of the best ways to stand out.*

42

Performing under pressure

First night nerves are nothing unusual for actors who use techniques to help them relax. Try these methods with your child to help him cope with potentially stressful situations.

Like actors preparing for auditions, children will face many situations where they're under pressure to perform. There are three things that will help them cope: preparation, preparation and ... preparation.

Actors relay many stories of how terrified they've been standing in front of casting directors, desperate to win a part. The audition process can be cruel and heartless. Just ask those poor people in floods of tears after hearing some harsh truths on TV talent shows. Even when an actor does get a job, the pressure continues to build. Will the other actors like them? How will they handle first night nerves, press night, oh, and yes, that evening when a coach-load of family and friends descend on the theatre to lend 'moral support'? An actor copes with pressure by warming-up thoroughly and concentrating her mind on the task ahead. She learns to ignore, as best she can, any outside distractions.

Here's an idea for you... **Try inventing a mantra to help calm your child's nerves. These are brilliant for helping a person remain focused and actors use them all the time. A rhyming four-line mantra can be fun to compose. How about 'I am relaxed, I am strong, and in spelling tests I'm never wrong'. Good, eh? Tell your child to repeat the saying a few times before the test. It will help her to concentrate and feel more confident.**

These are techniques and skills your child can master too for when he feels nervous, harassed or put on the spot. These could be tests at school, a fall-out with friends or the feeling he cannot manage the amount of homework he's getting. With regular practice an 'actor's warm-up' can become part of your child's routine before he embarks on any-thing stressful. A performer will never miss a warm-up on stage before the show because it helps her to prepare mentally. In life, mistakes often happen if you're rushing around and not focused before doing something important.

There is a physical warm-up where your child crouches on the floor and imagines he's a toy. Very slowly get him to be a floppy teddy bear coming to life. Make sure he doesn't rush this, so the slower the better. Actually, about one minute is an ideal amount of time. His head should be the very last thing to come up. There are some other physical exercises you and your child can do together before he tackles something stressful if you're feeling up to it:

- Roll the shoulders forwards and backwards to remove any tension. Then roll them up to the ears and drop them loosely.
- Bend and straighten the knees to remove tension there too. Also, circle the wrists clockwise and then anti-clockwise.
- Tense the fingers as if you are a witch casting a magic spell and then relax one finger at a time.

As well as preparing the body, an anxious child can benefit from the kind of vocal warm-up popular with actors:

There will be many occasions when kids have to do difficult things on their own. Have a read through IDEA 37, *The solo performance*, for some tips.

Try another idea...

■ Get him to imagine he is chewing a sticky toffee and it's stuck in his teeth. This really warms up the jaw.

■ Make him screw up his face as small as he can and then to stretch it out as long as he can.

■ Can he pull the ugliest face ever? Can he smile and look charming?

■ Try breathing out and then reciting the alphabet, getting louder and louder.

All these physical and vocal exercises prepare the body and mind for something that requires a lot of concentration. Tell your child before embarking on something difficult to close his eyes for a few seconds and focus completely on the mission ahead. They should imagine themselves doing it confidently and think about how great they'll feel once it is all over and they're being congratulated or praised for their achievement.

Actors standing in the wings ready to go on will not talk to anyone because they are totally prepared and focused on when they need to be on stage. Children can copy this by not chatting away to friends and messing about immediately before an important test or event so their mind doesn't wander.

'Pressure is a word which is mis-used in our vocabulary. When you start thinking about pressure, it's because you've started to think about failure.'
TOMMY LASORDA,
former manager, LA Dodgers

Defining idea...

How did it go?

Q   **My daughter gets so nervous every Friday because her class must recite their times tables out loud and individually. She tells me that when she has to stand up her voice starts to shake and her legs wobble. What can she do to calm her nerves?**

A   *If your daughter's shaky voice is purely because she lacks confidence rather than because she doesn't know her times tables then the remedy is simple. She should practise her breath control. Try this at home. Tell her to imagine her breathing as a big balloon she must deflate every time she speaks. After deflating the breath she needs to inflate the balloon again. Practising at home with you will also boost her confidence in reciting anything out loud.*

Q   **Practising her breathing is fine but how can we stop her worrying about her wobbly legs when it's her turn to stand up?**

A   *This is where physical exercises are so useful. To relax the legs, a good exercise is for her to put her heels together with her toes turning outwards. Now ask her to bend and stretch her knees, like a comedy policeman. When you say 'stop' her knees must stay bent and she can look through her legs, imagining she's looking through a magic window. What can she see? If she tries this in the playground before the lesson it will highlight to her the difference between relaxed and wobbly legs and help her to get them at least slightly relaxed before the test.*

43

Exploring the text

Performers study their lines in detail to discover what motivates their characters. Your child can open up, share opinions and contribute ideas by discussing stories he's read.

An actor who's not a good reader and finds it hard to analyse the words he needs to learn will struggle to make a living.

At an audition the best actors can grab clues from the text about the type of character the casting director is looking for, even if the words have only been shoved into their hands minutes before they're asked to perform them. Is there any sign of a dialect or accent? Any clues as to when and where the speech is taking place? It's surprising just how much information can be gathered just by asking yourself some simple questions. When he enters the audition room an actor will appear perfect for the role. Children can benefit greatly from studying texts in the same way. By discussing a fiction or non-fiction book with your child you can really gauge his interest in a subject or a particular character. If you're enthusiastic about books he'll be encouraged to develop his own writing and reading skills. He'll enjoy your

Here's an idea for you...

Get your child to think about a fictional character she's similar to. How about Little Red Riding Hood or Snow White? What do they have in common? Get her to think about the story surrounding the character and ask if she would have done anything different if she had been in the story. She might not have eaten that apple which poisoned Snow White. Finally, ask her to create a different ending to the story. She could perform it with her friends or toys.

interpretations of stories and those silly character voices you do that really bring a tale to life. A word of warning, though: as he gets older he might start to find those voices rather annoying.

The more he reads the better sight-reader he'll become, which will help him in different subjects at school. He'll also probably lose any bad reading habits, such as sub-vocalisation. This is when a child needs to hear himself saying the words as he reads, rather than being able to read silently in his head. Sometimes children can feel under so much pressure to read that the magic of a story is lost. If you can get your child more excited about the content of books rather than just the actual words he'll have the confidence to try new titles and not return to the same ones again and again which he can read with ease.

Actors will examine closely every single piece of text they're given to work with. Thespians we've known will virtually pull their lines to bits like biology students dissecting a frog to ensure they understand exactly what the writer meant when he penned those words.

Such critical analysis becomes even more important if the writer is dead. What was the author's inspiration for the piece? Fierce debates still rage about why Shakespeare wrote what he did. Analysing stories and comparing books by different authors and even titles by the same person will make your child feel less inhibited about reading aloud in class and he'll want to discuss texts with the teacher. His vocabulary will also develop faster, which will make him a more confident speaker.

Reading and writing go together like, well pen and paper. Get some tips on helping your child become a more confident writer in IDEA 40, *Have you read the script?*

Try another idea...

If your child is struggling with a particular book at school, get him to tell you all about it when he comes home or at bedtime. Who are the main characters and what part do they play in the story? Who are the goodies and the baddies? Does your child know anyone who reminds him of a particular character in the book? Actually you can have these types of discussions anytime and anywhere. You could be driving to the shops, stuck in traffic or talking over the breakfast table. This exercise goes further than simply discussing and analysing stories. Your child will become more confident about expressing his own point of view on a whole range of subjects. Don't forget to visit your local library, where a magical world lies inside its walls. Libraries really welcome children and many have story-telling sessions specifically to help kids fall in love with books.

But don't stop at books. Many actors also get their inspiration from newspapers and magazines. What are you waiting for?

'Books, I found, had the power to make time stand still, retreat or fly into the future.'
JIM BISHOP, US journalist

Defining idea...

How did it go?

Q **My nine-year-old daughter is reading a classic book at school which she hates. She tells me she dreads English lessons because of this and doesn't join in class discussions. How can I make her more enthusiastic?**

A *Check to see if the book she's studying has ever been made into a theatre production, TV show or film. There might even be an audio version of the book read by a famous actor. Sometimes a story told through a different medium can appeal to a child. If you cannot find the story in any other form, spend some time with her talking about the characters and the plot to get her more enthused.*

Q **The book is about a group of people stuck on a desert island which I thought would have been interesting for her. How can I discuss this in a different context?**

A *I would imagine the issues in the book are all about how people relate to each other when they are stranded in such a difficult situation. Ask her some fun questions such as which one of her friends she would like to be stuck on a desert island with. Who would be in charge and how would they survive? Talk about how this differs from the book. It might give her some ideas to discuss in class.*

44

That's what friends are for, front and backstage

Stage productions are a huge team effort. Team-building drama games will teach your child how to work with and trust other people to achieve something everyone wants.

Imagine two actors having a blazing row moments before going on stage where, during the first scene, they must pucker up and kiss as two lovers.

Take your problems on stage and a performance can go horribly wrong. In an attempt to avoid such potentially explosive moments casting directors will assess an actor's personality at the audition stage. Some will even sit incognito in the waiting areas during castings to see how people interact with each other. Even the most fantastic actors can see their work dry up if they earn a reputation for being difficult

Here's an idea for you... **Next time your child has a couple of friends over, play a game of TV Channels. One is in charge of an imaginary remote control and two are the actors. The child with the controller will shout what he wants to watch. It might be a cookery programme or a cartoon and the two friends must work together to act out a show. After 30 seconds the viewer shouts out that he wants to change channels.**

to work with. In an industry where there are hundreds of unemployed actors competing for a limited number of roles it's important to be liked. It's therefore incredibly useful to know when to bite your tongue. Children are no different when it comes to deciding who they like and who they cannot stand in a group. They will naturally be drawn to kids they have something in common with and where there is natural chemistry. Yet if a class or team is to function properly it is much easier if everyone gets on.

When we're talking about building confidence it's important your child can at least mix with all the kids in her class. She will probably have a couple of best friends but difficulties will arise if she has problems working with a child she doesn't like for some particular, and often irrational, reason. A drama teacher can spot very early on where there might be tension and will make a special effort to mix the children up because this is one of the best ways kids make new friends.

If you are involved in a kid's club a great exercise is called Find A Partner. You tell the children to find someone similar to them. They might share the same shoe size or have the same colour eyes. This exercise breaks down initial barriers among children who might not otherwise have the confidence to approach kids they don't know or are wary of. Arguments between close friends can also be avoided if team work is encouraged.

Your child's confidence will increase if she widens her social circle. For some tips on this see IDEA 34, *New friends, new situations*.

Try another idea…

There is a really fun game called Hands Only, which involves some basic props placed on a table, maybe a plastic tea set, a pencil and a spoon. Your child stands in front of a mate with her hands behind her back. The friend then stands behind her and puts their hands through her arms so it looks like the arms belong to your child. The child in front must talk to the audience (her other friends) as if she's demonstrating how to make a cup of tea. Whilst she does all the talking, her friend behind is actually picking up and using the props despite not really being able to see what's going on. This can be extremely funny for those watching and taking part. Although this is a good exercise for really good friends to play it is also a perfect ice breaker if a group of children do not really know each other but have to work together as part of a team to get a particular job done.

Running a home must be a team effort to avoid chaos, and your child will feel more confident about her role within it if she's involved in the decision-making process. In the same way a cast of actors, the director and the technical crew will talk through together what they think will and won't work during rehearsals, it's important to let kids have their say. Children are also more likely to obey house rules if they can see they apply to everyone and that the chores are shared.

'The way a team plays as a whole determines its success. You may have the greatest bunch of individual stars but if they don't play together the club won't be worth a dime.'

Defining idea…

BABE RUTH, baseball player

How did
it go?

Q   **My son loves football and is the strongest player in his side but I was recently told by his coach that he struggles to play as part of a team. He prefers to try to take the glory and score all the goals. How can I improve his appreciation of his team mates?**

A   *Why not invite some of the other players over to your local park for a practice and a game? You could set up a match with different roles and different dynamics. How about a game with adults versus children? If he feels he's no longer the best player on the pitch he will have to rely more on his team mates to win.*

Q   **Sounds good in theory, but finding time to go down the park with all these kids is going to be difficult. Can I help the coach to introduce something at training?**

A   *There are many drama exercises and games that are specifically designed to encourage teamwork. One involves getting two teams of children in two straight lines. When the coach says 'Go' the boy at the front must pass a ball to the person behind him without using his hands or feet. The idea is to get the ball all the way along the line without dropping it. This is, of course, an adaptation of the Pass The Orange game popular in our house once the clock strikes midnight on New Year's Eve.*

45

Next! Why is life so unfair?

Only 7% of actors are working at any one time so performers live with constant disappointment. Children who are confident in themselves accept they can't always win.

We've all seen football managers ranting and raving on television about how their team was robbed by a bad refereeing decision. It's not pretty.

Children need to know it is great to win, but it's how they behave when they lose which can often say more about them as a person. Your child's popularity with her friends, and therefore her confidence, will increase if she doesn't whine when things go wrong or boast and show off when she comes out on top. No one likes to play with a bad loser or an arrogant winner. Actors learn to cope with rejection very early in their careers. Casting directors audition hundreds of hopefuls for one part and it can be quite stressful to attend numerous call-backs only to be told 'thanks, but no thanks' at the very last hurdle. To receive such bad news on a

Select a small prize like a sweet and tell the children to imagine they're stranded on a desert island and must create a scene around how they will survive. Suddenly you arrive as the Magic Sweet Bearer and the sweet you have in your hand has the power to transport them home. However, only one of them can have the sweet. The kids have one minute to decide who deserves to be saved.

regular basis would drive most of us to sulkily give this career the proverbial finger and look for another way to earn a living. Actors are different. They expect such emotional kicks in the teeth and try to look on the bright side. It would be extremely unprofessional to throw a massive strop at the casting director, especially as she could be working on another project the performer might be suitable for. Instead the actor will be proud he got as far as he did, will make a mental note of why other people were more successful and continue training so he gets further in the audition process next time. And there will be a next time.

Children can learn a lot from adopting the same attitude to rejection. A wise teacher friend of ours tells her kids when they're nervous not to worry too much. Even if they fail a trial for a team or a test they'll always learn something from the experience which they'll be able to use another time. Accepting they cannot always win is an important social skill for children to learn and is certainly linked to their self-confidence. You'll know whether your child is lagging behind her friends in this area by judging how she reacts when they're playing together and she does not get her own way. It can be good for children to experience rejection from time to time. It will usually spur them on to work harder.

At one drama class a few boys were sent to a local amateur theatre group to audition for parts in Charles Dickens' *Oliver Twist*. Every boy got a part, except one. His mother was mortified and told the teacher she did not want her son to attend any more auditions. The teacher reassured her that he needed to keep trying. A couple of months later he won a role in a new BBC adaptation of this classic novel. If he had won a part in the amateur version he wouldn't have been available for the BBC role. His cloud had a very shiny silver lining.

The director is never wrong in the theatre and your child needs to have the confidence to take responsibility for her own decisions. IDEA 17, *Don't argue with the director*, has more on this.

Try another idea…

Next time your child comes home from school fuming that she hasn't won the part she wanted in her class assembly, try not to show any disappointment yourself. Instead, work on ways together that she might win a bigger role next time. Ask her why the child who got the main speaking part was given the job. Maybe that kid is very good at projecting his voice? You can then practise with your child reading a school book clearly and loudly, and giving her the next assembly as a goal to strive towards. This is all about helping your child focus on doing better next time rather than dwelling on failure, just as a performer would after a disappointing audition. Actors believe their time will come – and it usually does.

'No matter how hard the loss, defeat might serve as well as victory to shake the soul and let the glory out.'

AL GORE

Defining idea…

201

How did it go?

Q   **My child always ends up crying and throwing tantrums on sports day if he loses a race. Are there any exercises that make it easier for him to deal with not winning?**

A   *Lots of drama games would work here. One physical exercise is Snakes In The Grass. Here you select one person to be the snake in the centre of the room. The other children must run from one end to the other without being caught by the snake. If they get caught they're out. By playing this and similar games with friends and family regularly your child will get used to losing gracefully.*

Q   **Good idea, but it could become hard work if my child throws an embarrassing strop every time he loses. Any tips to speed up the process of learning to lose?**

A   *In acting classes performers play many competitive games and there are varieties which work very well with children who may win one and lose another. Although it's hard to ignore a tantrum ask your child to help you spot the next losers in the game so he still feels involved.*

46

A problem shared is a problem halved

Many children are reluctant to discuss their problems. Try techniques championed by acting guru Stanislavski, who claimed the secret is to ask open questions such as Who? What? Where? When? and Why?

Cynics argue that a problem shared is a problem two people have got. That's not true, of course, and children need to be confident enough to talk openly about what's worrying them.

The so-called father of modern theatre, Constantin Stanislavski, claimed a belief in what you are doing is central to good acting. This means you must ask yourself what a character is doing, with whom, where and why? Actors share their personal experiences with each other because they might prove useful when developing their own character or someone else's. We remember when one male actor had to play a husband whose wife had been unfaithful. He had never personally experienced such betrayal but an older actor in the cast had. During a moving speech the emotionally-bruised thespian recalled how after being away for a long stint on tour

Here's an idea for you... **Kids love detective games. Ask one of your child's friends to sit in a chair. They are accused of stealing a cookie by Mr Bumble the baker. Another child plays detective but can only ask five questions based around who, what, why, where and when. 'Why do you have cookie crumbs on your shirt?' Depending on the answers that are given everyone, including the child playing Mr Bumble, must decide if the accused is guilty.**

he'd come home and walked in on his wife and her lover. He was able to discuss this incident openly and provide some useful insights. It made the entire scene much more real. Let's just say he was a bitter man.

If your child finds it difficult to open up there are drama exercises to encourage her to share her experiences and concerns. One family game is called Free Talk where everyone is given a list of subjects they can discuss. This is a great one for the car. If you're convinced your child is worried about something at school you can make the list quite specific. How about this for starters:

- Why I do/don't like school
- My most embarrassing moment
- My favourite person and why
- Something that makes me really angry
- Something that makes me really happy
- My best day ever
- My worst day ever
- My funniest experience
- And so on ...

By discussing a topic in a team situation, as actors do when they're developing characters, your child will begin to identify with the views of other people. She'll realise that some points of view are shared and she is not the only one to have been through a particular experience. Sometimes kids are more confident talking about their problems to their friends rather than their parents. If this is the case in your house you can play Free Talk when she has some pals around to play. If you discreetly busy yourself bringing drinks and food you might pick up some snippets of information which will help you solve your child's problems discreetly. This is a great way of getting to the root of an issue without pressurising your child.

She might also find it easier to write things down. You could ask her and her friends to put pen to paper and answer one of the topics on the Free Talk list. If they're reluctant to write anything you can start with a fun topic such as 'What I want to watch on TV tonight'. Once they have made some notes and shared them you can move on to more serious topics. These could be 'What I do and don't like about school' or 'Why I'm scared of the dark'. Gradually your child will open up and the game will evolve into a serious discussion in the same way an actor debates with the director what his character has endured or enjoyed.

Timing is everything in the theatre and the same is true when it comes to getting kids to discuss difficult topics. Even the most sociable child needs her own space occasionally so don't force her to talk about things if she's blatantly not ready or has just walked in the door after a busy day at school. Things can always wait.

A child's self-esteem can rise if they learn not to take things too seriously and put experiences into perspective. IDEA 32, *Knowing when to laugh or cry*, will help here.

Try another idea...

'If you show people the problems and you show people the solutions they will be moved to act.'
BILL GATES

Defining idea...

How did it go?

Q **My daughter always seems to have the weight of the world on her shoulders but when I ask her what's wrong she always replies 'nothing' and sits in her room alone. What should I do?**

A *For a start, stop asking her what's wrong. The next time you're together, tell her some of your past experiences at school – good and bad. How did you behave and who did you get on with? Remember that teacher who made your life a misery and the one you always felt you could talk to when you had a problem? Actors love the chance to regale each other with anecdotes of old. If you start to confide in your daughter she's more likely to open up to you.*

Q **We've tried this. She seems to be enjoying hearing my stories but she still isn't telling me what's bothering her. What more can we do?**

A *Try the writing it down approach. Ask her to design a little shield of her life. You can divide the shield into sections and label them as things she likes, things she hates, her favourite people, best day of the week, worst day of the week and so on. Actors will often do exercises like this to help them develop a layered character. It should help your daughter to express herself and give you more of an idea of how she's feeling so she has the confidence to deal with difficulties in her life.*

47

That's history. Period!

Actors love playing characters from the past. By discussing historical scenes with your child he'll notice how society has changed and the days of kids being seen and not heard are long gone.

Whether it's the roaring 20s, medieval England or the Wild West, we all love stories of romance or bloodthirsty villains from a bygone age.

Actors dream of landing a lead role in a high-budget period drama with its larger than life characters, elaborate costumes and powerful storylines. It seems the chance to fight with swords, attend a royal ball at the palace or die an untimely death by torture is too big an opportunity for any ambitious thespian to turn down. One director remembers how he helped an actress really 'feel' the character of a Victorian lady by insisting she wore a corset during the rehearsal process. Such was the constricting nature of the garment that our actress could hardly breathe. At the end of the show the director remarked how he'd never seen her act so well.

Here's an idea for you... **Discover who your child's favourite character from history is and create a short story featuring him as that figure. You act as a narrator and pause during the story-telling to let your child act out the leading role. He could be David killing Goliath. You could even invite some of his friends to a themed meal.**

Spare a thought for the poor researchers who dare not make any mistakes with the sets, scripts or costumes. If they do, they can expect a flood of letters from irate members of the public pointing out basic flaws. After all, give a soldier in a play about the First World War a weapon that was not invented for another thirty years and he'll have a huge unfair advantage.

For children, a period drama can be a hugely creative and rewarding learning experience as their general knowledge expands. Actors study Greek, Italian and Elizabethan theatre when they're training to understand how plays were performed in the era they were written for. Getting children to act out Greek myths can be great fun. Does your child realise we're still surrounded by evidence of ancient Greece? Look at the star constellations or watch the Olympics. Then there are those fantastic stories about monsters and gods that will set their pulses racing.

Children may have heard the expression 'He's got the Midas touch', but do they know it relates to the story about a king who makes a wish that everything he touches turns to gold? The moral, of course, is to be careful what you wish for and not be greedy. Once you've told the story to your child and his friends they could act it out and even make costumes. Bed sheets and some string is all that's needed here. Imagine how proud he'll feel when he tells his teacher he knows the story of King Midas. Not only has he heard a great tale and made and worn fun costumes, he's learned something, too.

You can do a similar thing if your daughter dreams of being a princess or a queen. Why not spend some time researching past queens who will capture her imagination? There's Cleopatra, Elizabeth I or even Boadicea – the warrior queen. Now there's a great example of girl power from one amazingly confident woman. Again, you can have hours of fun making costumes and putting on make-up to re-create these famous historical characters who your child will love and never forget.

There is a really fun period-based drama game children enjoy. It's called Off With Your Head, a saying made famous by the Queen in *Alice in Wonderland* and also associated with a certain Henry VIII. One at a time the children must stand up and tell a made-up story about why they weren't responsible for stealing the King's new crown. They can really stretch their imagination for this one and come up with some brilliant excuses. Once all the kids have a turn everyone must vote for the best story to set that child free. The rest get chants of 'Off with your head'.

Whatever era you choose, try to get some relevant books or television dramas out on DVD from the library to see how different periods and historical characters have been portrayed by actors over the years.

Try another idea…

Letting your child be different characters is a great way to illustrate how everyone is different. IDEA 16, *Building your own character*, explores this in detail.

Defining idea…

'History ought never to be confused with nostalgia. It's written not to revere the dead, but to inspire the living.'

SIMON SCHAMA, author of *A History of Britain*

How did it go?

Q **This all sounds great but my knowledge of history is very limited; how can I help my child if I'm not sure of the historical facts myself?**

A *Once you've established what period in history your child is interested in or studying at school, find out who he likes from that era. Is it a goodie or a baddie? At home you can carry out some research together into that person online or at the library. What did that person eat? What was his or her family like? Did they meet a tragic end? Are they famous for anything unusual? You will find that your own knowledge and confidence in history develops.*

Q **How can I avoid making mistakes that might conflict with what he is learning at school?**

A *To avoid this you can ask your child to list the characteristics of the historical figure he's learning about in class. Once you have assembled this information you can ask him to tell you about the period in history and base a little play or speech around the facts he already knows. This will help him absorb all the information he's already learnt and build up his confidence as he suddenly realises he knows more than you!*

48

Birthdays can bring happy returns

Children's birthday parties can be stressful and expensive. Yet take some magic make-believe, choose the right theme and costumes, and watch your child's celebration turn into the perfect confidence booster.

Rather than waiting tables these days, out-of-work actors prefer to take their lives in their hands and host hectic birthday bashes for kids.

Magicians and clowns are so last century. The trend today is for birthday parties to combine a massive helping of fun with a huge dollop of confidence-boosting drama and dancing games. These shindigs are often run by actors who, let's just say, are between jobs right now. Children can choose the theme. How about Witches and Wizards, Princesses or Superheroes? It goes without saying that everyone (including Mum and Dad!) needs to dress up. Drama games are played to inspire the kids and keep them entertained. They are structured in such a way that shy children love them and feel more confident after taking part. The actor will often encourage the kids to work on their own mini-script which they can perform when their parents pick them up. Acting games are the perfect way to break the ice and get a party started. An actor will almost certainly want to play some of his favourite physical

A great exercise for your child's birthday is called Magic Spot. Ask your child and his friends to decorate a large cardboard circle. Tell them this is a magical spot and when they stand on it they will behave in a certain way. It might make them giggle or unable to speak. If they stand on it and the spot works they win a prize. The spot might make them itch uncontrollably or talk very loudly. Quiet children find this exercise fun as it distracts from their nerves and gives them a focus to achieve.

warm-up exercises, which can be tweaked to suit the chosen theme.

Here's one. Once the children have settled in, ask them to stand in a big circle. You walk around the outside and give each child one of three different names. If it is a pirate party you could use One-Eyed Jack, Wooden Leg Bill or Black Skull Bob. You then call out one name. If it's One-Eyed Jack all the kids with that name must run clockwise around the circle. If you call 'Change!' they must change direction and if you shout 'Home!' they must return to their place in the circle. The last child back is out and sits down. You then repeat this with the other two names and continue until you have a winner from each group who wins a prize. The final element of the party, after the themed food of course, can be rehearsing the mini-script. The actor will know how important it is to keep things simple and will ensure every child has a line to say.

Let's stick with the pirate idea for this one. The bandits could come marching in behind their captain (the birthday boy) and start digging for treasure. Perhaps the captain has to take the pirate register to check all his ship-mates are there. The children can think up silly names for their characters. The scene could end with the crew finding a hidden gem and performing a party dance to celebrate. Whatever theme you choose, your child will grow in confidence because in his mind he is playing rather than performing. His party will be talked about for weeks afterwards by his friends and their parents who were impressed by the end performance.

Drama parties also work well if the children create their own show. IDEA 15, *Improvisation means imagination*, has some tips on how to make up an original story.

Try another idea…

Here's a quick checklist to ensure your drama party goes with a bang.

- Make sure the venue is big enough.
- Think of a theme your child   his guests will enjoy.
- Make your own invites and request that the kids dress appropriately.
- Decorate the room to suit the theme and find fitting music.
- Prepare food that is relevant to the theme. Gold chocolate coins go down a blast with budding pirates.

You don't have to wait until it's your child's birthday to have a confidence-enhancing drama party. If you've recently moved home, why not invite some of his new classmates for a house warming? Or you could use another event, such as Halloween, as the perfect excuse, especially as there is a ready-made theme.

'I am thankful for the mess to clean after a party because it means I have been surrounded by friends.'
NANCIE J. CARMODY, humourist

Defining idea…

How did
it go?

Q **I love the idea of having a themed party for my daughter's eighth birthday but I cannot afford an actor to host it. Unfortunately my own script-writing skills are terrible. Do you have any suggestions?**

A *If preparing a script terrifies you then wait until the big day and devise a story then. You can always think of a great idea beforehand. Your child and her friends could be in different pop bands battling to win a talent show? They could choreograph their own short dance routine to some music they all like and act out a scene of them preparing to go on stage. If your daughter is too shy to be in one of the bands she could always be a judge.*

Q **The party is supposed to be two hours long. What if I run out of games and ideas?**

A *The knack here is to research and write down a list of games you can play before party day. There are so many children's party games that you won't have any trouble finding ones she'll like. Especially if she helps you choose them. She'll know better than you which ones her and her friends would really like to play. There are lots of new games linked to drama training as well as classics such as Musical Chairs, Pin The Tale On The Donkey and the old favourite Pass The Parcel. Two hours will fly by.*

49

Audience participation

Some people cower in their seats at the thought of being dragged on stage. But volunteering has its advantages if your child is confident enough to put up her hand.

Love it or hate it, reality TV gives ordinary people a brief encounter with fame. For most of us though, the thought of being so publicly scrutinised makes us feel physically sick.

The phrase 'audience participation' can split a nation; there's no doubt about it. Behind every eager beaver stretching their arm to the sky in the theatre and calling 'Me, me!' when the call for volunteers goes up, there's always someone behind them trying their hardest not to be noticed. Go along to any acting class and the participants will be almost fighting amongst themselves to be chosen for an exercise or demonstration. They want the teacher or director to be aware of them and they realise that doing is much better than watching when it comes to learning a new acting technique. Many shows encourage audience participation because it adds colour, fun and a level of unpredictability to a performance. We might hate to admit it, but seeing someone's dad humiliated on stage and covered in some horrid

Here's an idea for you... **A subtle way to build a child's confidence so they can lead a game is to play Old Man's Footsteps. One child plays the old man and stands at one end of the room with his back to everyone else. The rest of the children stand in a straight line at the opposite end and must creep up on the old man. When he turns around everyone must freeze. If he sees anyone moving that person must go back to the start. The first child to reach the old man must shout 'old man's footsteps' and they become the old man.**

green liquid for getting a question wrong is quite amusing in a sadistic kind of way.

The benefits to your child of volunteering can be immense. She'll learn first-hand how to do something rather than simply observing. In fact, she might get the chance to try something her friends do not, or to visit a place she would otherwise never get near at her age. These are all experiences that will increase her self-esteem. Some children just need an initial burst of confidence to raise their hand and then they're away, putting themselves forward for anything and everything.

There are some good exercises you can perform with your child to get her into the habit of volunteering. The trick is to start slowly with low-pressure games. If an activity is really fun, taking part becomes irresistible. These exercises also work best if your child is unaware you have any expectations of her at all. The best time to play these drama games is when there are friends or family visiting. Perhaps it's the type of family gathering where traditionally your child has been reluctant to participate and would spend much of the time doing his own thing?

A good starter is Wink Murder. Everyone sits in a circle and you ask for a volunteer to be the 'detective'. Your child might not push himself forward straightaway, but don't worry. The detective must leave the room while a 'murderer' is selected. The detective then re-enters the room and the murderer must wink at people in the circle to kill them. The victims must fall to the floor in dramatic style (this is something actors milk for all it's worth when they play this game). The idea is for the detective to guess who the assassin is. If he or she is successful they remain the officer and leave the room again while another murderer is chosen. If the murderer is not discovered a new detective is found. This game can have even the shyest children desperate to have a go at being the policeman.

There is another drama game ideal for encouraging volunteering which requires the chosen child to wait outside the room. Everyone remaining inside must think of a descriptive word or an adjective. Good choices are 'loudly', 'happily' or 'slowly'. When the volunteer comes back into the room she asks everyone else to do three things in the style of the chosen word. Maybe dance, walk or individually introduce themselves. After the third request she must try to guess the word.

Once again this game can be so alluring and tempting for children, and your child will realise how she can have more fun by volunteering than remaining in the background.

Volunteering takes guts and can mean taking risks. IDEA 41, *Daring to be different*, gives some pointers on how to encourage your child to do something daring occasionally.

Try another idea...

'I think of life itself now as a wonderful play that I've written for myself, and so my purpose is to have the utmost fun playing my part.'
SHIRLEY MACLAINE

Defining idea...

How did it go?

Q I'm taking my child to a Christmas show where kids are always invited on to the stage at the end. I would love my child to be chosen because the volunteers are given presents. Should I encourage her to put herself forward?

A *Only if she's really keen to get on stage. If she is, you can speak to the front of house manager when you arrive at the theatre. Nowadays volunteers are often arranged at the start of the performance to save time during the show. If your daughter is reluctant to take part don't force her. If this is her first theatre trip she may wish to watch other kids taking part this time and she'll realise just how much fun it is.*

Q What if she gets up on stage but then refuses to participate?

A *Don't worry about that. Children's entertainers and actors are fantastic at dealing with all kinds of youngsters whether they're very loud or very quiet kids. Even if your child doesn't say much make sure you reassure her afterwards that she was very brave. Volunteering for anything is a huge achievement.*

50

There's no such word as can't

Your child's confidence can be dented if he finds something difficult. Kids need to analyse daunting tasks in the same way actors spend time 'finding' their characters.

Actors are urged to say yes to everything. We know one actress who pretended she could ride a bike to win a role. Watching a 26-year-old on stabilisers weeks before rehearsals was a sight to behold.

Like all performers she has an insatiable appetite for trying new things, however hard they may appear. It would be easy for an actor to shy away from a heavy classical script, fearing she'd be out of her depth. Instead, she'll know from years of training that by researching the character and studying the text she can achieve something that looks unattainable. Your child will also benefit if he has the confidence to try things that he would prefer to avoid altogether.

Acting out proverbs is a fun way to explain to children how their confidence will grow if they never give up. There are many sayings such as 'Nothing ventured, nothing gained' or 'If at first you don't succeed, try, try again'. Ask your child to act a scene around one of the sayings. He could be a gardener whose plants keep dying but eventually he grows the tallest sunflower in the world.

Actors search for creative ways to solve problems, and kids can too. If a thespian is struggling with a role he'll explore his character's predicament. Dustin Hoffman spent months researching autism to polish up his part in the 1988 movie *Rain Man*.

Here's an exercise you can try with your child. It's called Anything Is Possible. Ask him to think of something he would be unable to do. He might say he could never climb the tallest building in the world. Get him to act out trying to reach the top. He can even pretend to have magic wings so he can float down when he reaches the roof. Other scenarios include taming a vicious lion to turn it into a friendly cat or building a machine that can do his homework. Although these examples are extremes they'll show him how he can be creative to solve problems and ultimately come out on top. This will help him view real challenges as potentially rewarding and fun rather than impossible. Actors perform scenes and lines in many different styles during rehearsals. Often they'll look and feel rather silly and make mistakes but these are all obstacles to overcome on the bumpy road towards accomplishing something new.

When you do drama exercises with your child part of the fun can be the hilarious results you all witness when things do go wrong. Don't worry. This is all about gradually building up your child's confidence so he doesn't worry so much about failing. Instead he'll become even more determined to keep going and going until he conquers a task. Try this game called Number Actions. Two children (or you and your child) face each other and count up to three alternating who says which numbers until you are both confidently counting quickly. When you feel ready replace the number two with a stamp of the foot and carry on. Then replace 'three' with a clap of the hand so the sequence is 'one, stamp, clap'. The final trick is to substitute 'one' with the word 'yeah'. Expect more than a fit of giggles for this one. This is a game which can take ages to get right. It can become infuriating for your child, but hopefully he'll be having such a great time he won't want to stop until you both crack it. This is both a mentally and physically challenging game so don't play it only the once. Try it every few days so your child sees how he's getting quicker and better at something which he struggled to get right when you first started.

There is another acting technique you can adopt if your child is struggling to understand something at school. If spelling is proving difficult, make some actor-style 'prompt' cards and test him each night before bed. Many performers claim this is one of the most effective ways to learn lines.

Whatever the task, remember to congratulate your child on the progress he's making in something he thought he'd never do.

Try another idea…

If you and your child are getting frustrated with something he's finding difficult have a read through IDEA 38, *Confidence is a gradual process*, because small improvements are actually major achievements.

Defining idea…

'The biggest problem is getting beyond the "you can't" syndrome. The moment you figure that out, you're on your way to flying. All the problems sitting there are an invitation for you to be creative.'
BILL DRAYTON, social entrepreneur

How did
it go?

Q **My son is convinced he can't tell the time and has given up even trying. Do you have any ideas to spur him on?**

A *Learning to tell the time becomes easier if it is made fun. Familiarise your child with clocks and listen to them chime and tick. How many toys can he pick up in five minutes? Can he get washed and put on his pyjamas before the big hand strikes the twelve? There is also the old favourite of What's The Time Mr Wolf? Ask your child to be the wolf and you chant the words, 'What's the time Mr Wolf?' The wolf mentions a wrong time, prompting you to repeat the chant and creep closer. When he tells the right time he gets to chase you. Oh yes, also put a watch on his wrist!*

Q **What if he can't tell the time at all? Won't he become frustrated playing these types of games?**

A *You can switch roles with you playing the wolf so your child starts to recognise the time. Rather than saying the exact time as the wolf you could say: 'The big hand is on the 12 and the little hand is on the 6'. Have patience. You can also get him to copy a clock from one of his favourite storybooks and decorate it with characters as well as numbers on the face.*

When sorry seems to be the hardest word

By using tried and tested acting techniques your child will have the confidence to accept when she's wrong and consider alternative ways to deal with difficult situations.

If an actor fluffs his lines on stage he's expected to say sorry to those in that scene at the end of the show. If he doesn't he'll be branded unprofessional behind his back.

We all make mistakes and, let's be really honest, we've all blamed someone else for one of our own misdemeanours. Or is that just us? In the theatre, once an actor has acknowledged he got it wrong the slate is wiped clean. Everyone can go about their usual business without resentment building up within the cast, which can put a big fat dampener on everyone's morale. Your child will earn the respect of others if she has the confidence to admit when she's wrong and can apologise. Actors have an uncanny ability to express their feelings freely. They're encouraged during their

Here's an idea for you...

Every kid has to say sorry sometimes so highlight this with a game of Can I Have A Quick Word. Your child must think of a situation where a person in authority could be wrong. Maybe the shop owner has sold some food that's gone off? Get him to act out being the person who has made the mistake and you're the one complaining. The scene should result in a sincere apology rather than an argument. Your child will see how things can be resolved.

training to face up to their demons and not bottle up their emotions. Tension or anxieties in any group situation becomes heavy baggage on a performer's back when he's trying to develop a believable character.

So what about kids? There's a school of thought that children actually use the word 'sorry' far too often. They will say it when they're told to just to keep adults happy. So do they really mean it? In our house if a child does something wrong, we'll ask them what they're actually apologising for. The results can be quite enlightening because it really does make them think about what they've done. Of course, we don't want to create a situation where we're all persistently apologising just to keep the peace. Kids must be confident enough to make a noise or create a mess without the fear of always being reprimanded.

There is a useful exercise actors use to free their minds if they're feeling guilty about something. It's called Doing Things Differently and you can play it at home to encourage your child to admit her mistakes. Each person must think of something they've done in their lives which they now regret. Your child may have been horrible to a friend, copied someone's homework or taken a sweet from the shop when she thought no one was looking. You can start off with minor admissions to get the exercise going. Maybe it was you who took the last biscuit from the jar last night? If you're all in the mood to explore this idea further you can create a short play featuring one or more of the regrets. The twist is you must give each situation a different – more positive – ending. This will help your child to get closure on something that might be bothering her because she can act out what she now wishes had really happened at the time. Don't worry if you prefer not to actually perform. Just having an exchange of views can give your child the confidence to act differently next time. Actors spend ages in these kinds of group debates when they're exploring their character's life and relationships.

Children will be criticised for their mistakes so being able to handle disapproving comments is a useful skill. IDEA 7, *Lovely darling, but ...*, gives some hints on this.

Try another idea...

You can adapt this exercise to help your child solve a specific problem she's going through right now. Maybe she's had a huge row with her best buddy and just needs the confidence to admit she was wrong and to say sorry. Ask her to think of how she could have dealt with the original problem differently and what she wishes she'd said. You could try role-playing the scene with you taking the part of the friend. The action will probably end with you both apologising to each other. Once your child realises how much better she feels once she admits she has made a mistake and moves on, she'll be more confident to deal with a similar situation if it occurs again.

'You can't spend your whole life apologising. Your responsibility is to show you've learned from it. Then move on and don't do it again.'

JUDE LAW, actor

Defining idea...

How did
it go?

Q   My son used to play with the boy next door all the time but they argued at the park and are both refusing to say sorry. What should I do?

A   *Children can be reluctant to say sorry because they feel embarrassed and it means admitting they were wrong. Ask your child to list the good things he likes about his friend and recall fun experiences they've had together. The next time you see his friend your child could remind him of one of those funny experiences to break the ice. Looking on the funny side of things can calm even the most difficult situations.*

Q   What if my son's friend refuses to accept the apology? Won't this really knock his confidence?

A   *Make sure he knows it takes a really big person to say sorry and even if his apology falls on deaf ears he has done the right thing. If you've encouraged your child to express his feelings during this whole process, at least he'll have gained in confidence to speak up for himself. When an actor makes a blunder in the theatre he must mentally wipe out the incident from his head so he can concentrate on the rest of the show. Tell your son that now he has apologised he must forget about what happened. Help him to focus on something else by taking him for a pizza.*

Smile for the camera, please

All actors need a professional photo before a casting director will see them. Children can get a real confidence boost by pampering themselves with a photo session and seeing the end result.

Every picture tells a story and actors know their photograph is one of their most important sales tools if they're to win that great role.

An actor will make the best use of what he's got for a professional photo rather than trying to fool the camera. If he looks like a villain or as if his face needs a jolly good iron he could go to the top of the pile for those really gritty parts. Actors spend ages preparing for their head shot. They must look good as well as providing casting directors with an honest representation. After all, this is not some sordid dating website where people can hide behind the image of a supermodel or an airline pilot. They'd soon be found out at the audition. Whether an actor loves or

Here's an idea for you... **Give your child and her friends a disposable or digital camera to make a photo story with speech bubbles. Keep the story short, with maybe five pictures. Make sure they write a brief script and everyone plays a character they are happy with. The children can make costumes and construct the set. They can add the speech bubbles to the pictures later or use computer technology to create a magazine-style photo story.**

loathes having his picture taken, he must be comfortable in front of the camera. A successful session with a good photographer can be a massive fillip to his confidence. If you look good, you feel good.

Most children love cameras, and taking and being in pictures can be a wonderful way to give them the boost they need when they're feeling down. Digital cameras aren't that expensive nowadays and you can buy disposable cameras for a few pounds in the high street. A great idea is to give your child a pamper day where the end result is a selection of gorgeous or handsome photos, both serious and silly. You can help her prepare for the 'shoot' by spending time making sure she looks her best. On some films, actors are asked to try on different clothes and wear their hair in a selection of styles. Select some of her favourite party clothes or dig deep among that pile of dressing-up costumes stuffed under her bed. Next choose a plain back-drop in the house or use the garden. Ask her to think up some different poses for the camera. If you're stuck for ideas, copy the poses used by celebrities in magazines. After the shoot you can have the photos developed or upload them immediately on to your computer. Together you can select the best ones to blow up as gifts for friends and family. The compliments will come flying in. If there's a really funny picture you could get it developed as a poster for her bedroom.

She can also get a confidence boost by being her own photographer. She could take pictures of her favourite pet or one of her friends. If you're attending an event, give her a camera so she can make her own photo-diary. She could even host her own exhibition when family or friends visit. Photography is also a great way to get your child more involved in the family holiday. She'll become more observant about what's going on in a particular location if she has been put in charge of keeping a record of the trip. You can help her by noting areas of interest. This is not just about pointing a camera and pressing a button. She is making crucial decisions about what to snap and what to ignore. By letting your child express her creativity in this way, she'll look forward to seeing the results of her efforts and showing other people her work. If she's usually very shy about talking to people then having some pictures to show can spark conversations.

An actor will acquire many photos which are often the only mementos of roles he's played and costumes he's worn. He will treasure these shots which have shaped his career and his life, so encourage your child to make albums of these happy times too.

Try another idea…

Actors love putting on costumes and children adore dressing up and painting their faces. These little extras will enhance any photo session so take a peek at IDEA 11, Dressing the part, make-up and all.

Defining idea…

'It takes a lot of imagination to be a good photographer. You need less imagination to be a painter because you can invent things. But in photography everything is so ordinary; it takes a lot of looking before you learn to see the ordinary.'

DAVID BAILEY

How did it go?

Q **My child loves taking photos, but the thought of giving her our expensive camera to take pictures does not fill my husband with joy. Disposable cameras rarely produce good quality pictures so what should we do?**

A   *If your child has an interest in photography it would be a shame not to encourage it. Despite what you might think about disposable cameras, the technology has moved on significantly in recent years. The days of foggy, out-of-focus pictures are long gone. Many of these box cameras now have an in-built flash and some are even waterproof. Another solution is to organise a photo session with your child that your husband can be closely involved with. This way he can supervise how his expensive digital camera is used.*

Q **My child gets very shy when she's having her school photo taken and ends up scowling at the camera. Will we ever be able to get a nice shot of her in her uniform?**

A   *We know a lot of actors who practice their 'photo' face in the mirror to avoid dodgy shots. Why not prepare your daughter for her next school photo by rehearsing the faces she will present? If she can see how pretty she looks when she smiles she'll be more inclined to grin for the photographer when the time comes.*

The end ...

Or is it a new beginning?

We hope the ideas in this book will have inspired you to use drama as a fun way to encourage your child to be more outgoing. Hopefully you've been able to see gradual improvements in your child's confidence, social skills and willingness to take part. Perhaps you've even enjoyed some of the exercises and games yourself.

So why not let us know all about it. Tell us how you got on. What really helped your child come out of his shell? Maybe you've got some tips of your own you want to share (see next page if so). And if you liked this book you may find we have even more brilliant ideas that could change other areas of your life for the better.

You'll find the Infinite Ideas crew waiting for you online at www.infideas.com.

Or if you prefer to write, then send your letters to:
Boost Your Child's Confidence
The Infinite Ideas Company Ltd
36 St Giles, Oxford, OX1 3LD, United Kingdom

We want to know what you think, because we're all working on making our lives better too. Give us your feedback and you could win a copy of another *52 Brilliant Ideas* book of your choice. Or maybe get a crack at writing your own.

Good luck. Be brilliant.

Offer one

CASH IN YOUR IDEAS

We hope you enjoy this book. We hope it inspires, amuses, educates and entertains you. But we don't assume that you're a novice, or that this is the first book that you've bought on the subject. You've got ideas of your own. Maybe our authors have missed an idea that you use successfully. If so, why not put it in an e-mail and send it to: yourauthormissedatrick@infideas.com, and if we like it we'll post it on our bulletin board. Better still, if your idea makes it into print we'll send you four books of your choice or the cash equivalent. You'll be fully credited so that every-one knows you've had another Brilliant Idea.

Offer two

HOW COULD YOU REFUSE?

Amazing discounts on bulk quantities of Infinite Ideas books are available to corpo-rations, professional associations and other organisations.

For details call us on:
+44 (0)1865 514888
fax: +44 (0)1865 514777
or e-mail: info@infideas.com

Where it's at ...